LISTON

ALI

MUHAMMAD ALI

igloobooks

igloobooks
Published in 2014
by Igloo Books Ltd
Cottage Farm
Sywell
NN6 0BJ
www.igloobooks.com

The measurements used are approximate.

Writen by Louise Spilsbury

SHE001 0714
2 4 6 8 10 9 7 5 3 1
ISBN 978-1-78440-005-7

Printod and manufactured in China

CONTENTS

MUHAMMAD ALI

Muhammad Ali is probably the most famous boxer of all time and one of the most recognised athletes in the world. When he was still a skinny child with just one win under his belt, he started to boast about being the greatest, but he soon backed up his brash claims with ability, dedication and expertise, and proved them to be true. Ali was the first man to win the undisputed World Heavyweight boxing title three times and he beat more champions and top contenders than any other heavyweight champion in history.

At the height of his fame, Ali had it all. He was young, strong, handsome and charismatic. He enraged opponents and entertained fans with his arrogant proclamations and witty pre-match taunts. He lit up the ring with his quick reflexes, strong punches and unique fighting style: a style that went against many of the game's fundamental teachings. As well as being a sporting legend, Ali is almost as well-known for his actions outside the ring, as a thinker, poet and an artist.

The story of Muhammad Ali's long, successful life has all the drama, twists and turns of a movie script. His boxing career began with a chance encounter that would seem far-fetched if it weren't true. He wanted to be loved, but he never shied away from controversy. His conversion to Islam, his fights for civil rights, and his outspoken condemnation of and refusal to fight in the Vietnam War surrounded him with controversy for many years. Even after he retired from the ring, he stayed in the public eye through charitable work and humanitarian missions around the world. Muhammad Ali was and is simply a man no one could ignore.

"I am the greatest. I said that even before I knew I was."
Muhammad Ali

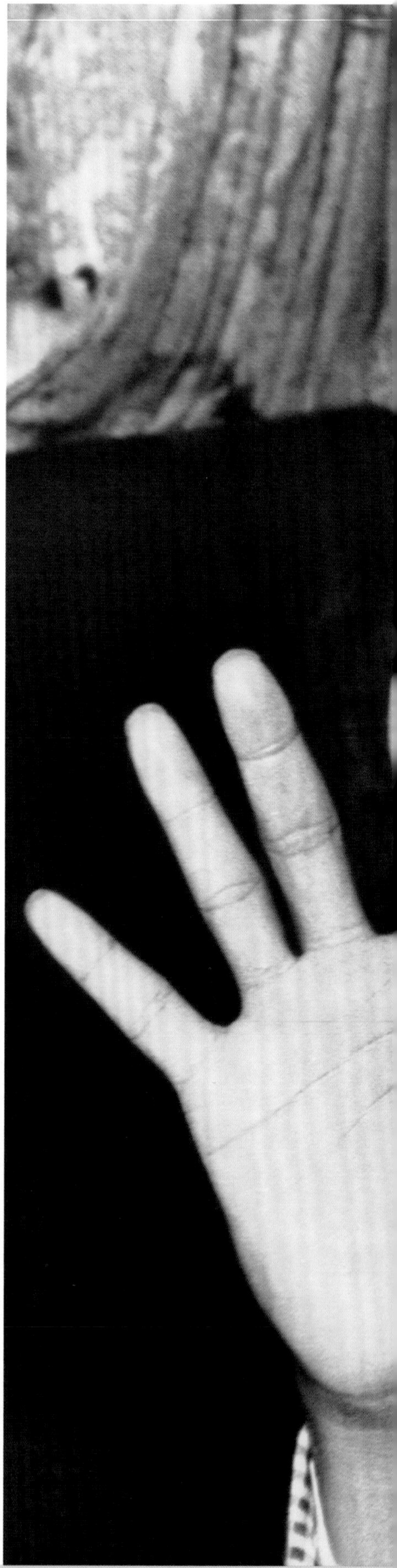

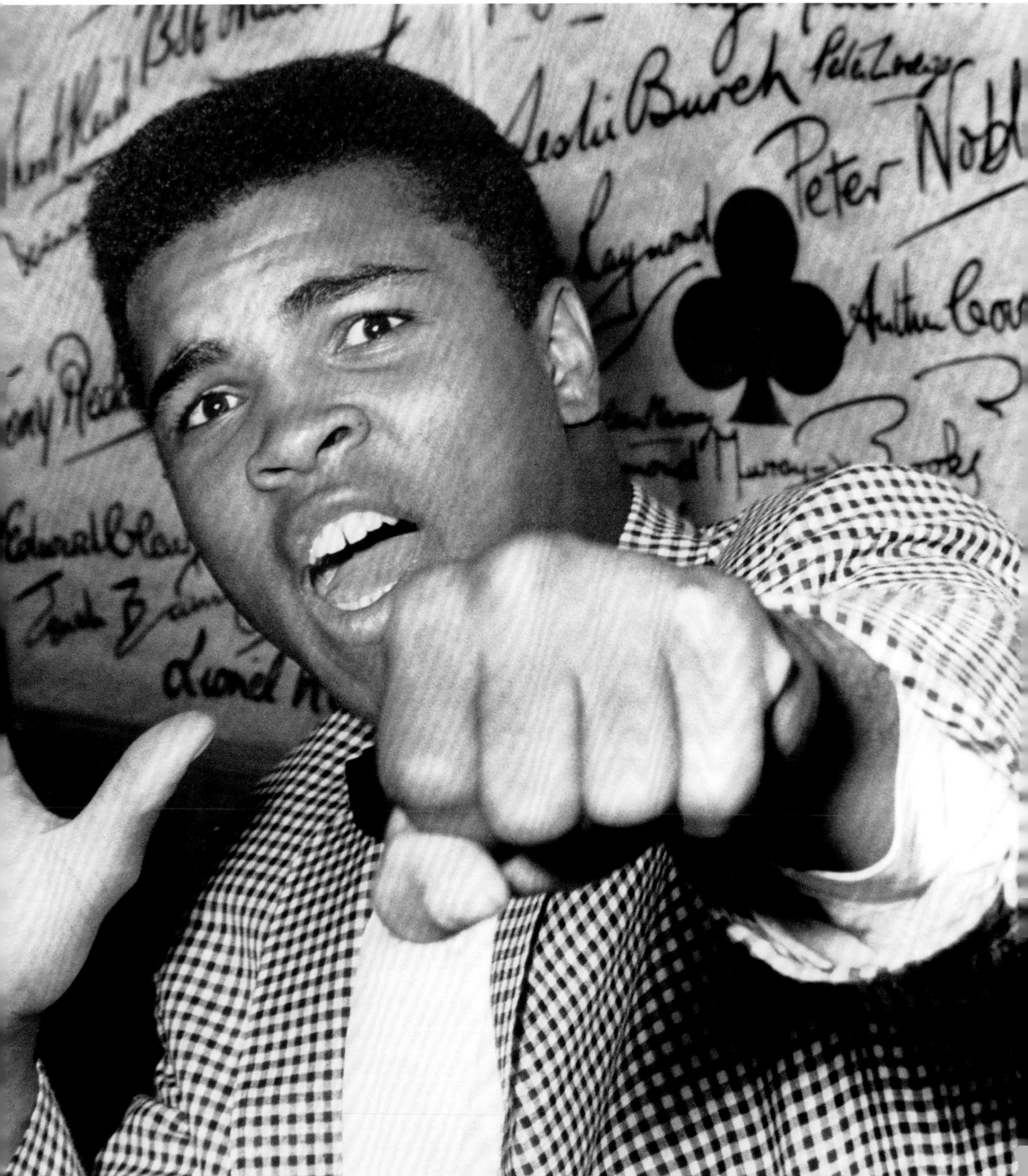

EARLY YEARS

Clay always called his mother "Mama Bird" because when he was young he said he thought she had a tiny, little bird nose. "I don't know why I thought that, because birds don't have noses, but from the moment I said it we all started calling her Mama Bird." Here he is seen fooling around with his mother in Pittsburgh, Pennsylvania, in 1963.

CASSIUS CLAY, JR

Muhammad Ali was born at 6:35 p.m. on 17 January 1942. At the first of many weigh-ins during his life, he was just 6 pounds, 7 ounces (2.92 kg). He was named Cassius Marcellus Clay, Jr., after his father, Cassius Marcellus Clay, Sr. His mother was Odessa Grady Clay. Two years after Cassius was born, his younger brother, Rudolph or Rudy (later Rahman Ali) joined the family.

All of Clay's four grandparents were free people, but his ancestors were slaves during the pre-Civil War era in the American South. Cassius Marcellus Clay, Sr. was named after Cassius Clay, the 19th century abolitionist who owned slaves but was also one of the first to set them free. Two of Cassius's paternal great-grandparents had been his slaves. His mother's paternal grandfather was Abe Grady, a white Irishman who emigrated to the United States soon after the Civil War and married a freed slave. Her maternal grandparents were a white man named Thomas Morehead and a slave.

Odessa was born in Kentucky, but moved to Louisville with her mother and siblings after her parents separated. Times were tough and she had to work to buy her own clothes so that she could go to school. She met Cassius's father when she was 16 years old. Cassius Marcellus Clay, Sr. was a muralist and painter, but earned a living painting billboards and signs. Odessa worked while the children were very young, as a house cleaner and a cook. The Clays weren't rich but they worked hard to bring up the boys in the best street they could afford. They lived at 3302 Grand Avenue, a small, four-roomed house in an all-black neighbourhood in Louisville, Kentucky. Clay remembered a mostly happy and loving home with his father always hugging and kissing him and Rudy, and his mother as a kind, gentle person.

Odessa Clay wipes down her son following a training bout in 1974. She was a calm, kind influence on him throughout her life.

CASSIUS AS A KID

As befits one of the world's great storytellers, there are many childhood tales about Clay. His mother started to call him 'GG' when he was a baby because that was the sound he made from his crib. When Clay became a Golden Gloves champion, he said of his first words, "You know what that meant? I was trying to say Golden Gloves." Odessa also used to tell people proudly that her eldest's first knockout punch was at six months old when he hit her and loosened two teeth so badly that she had to have them pulled out. Rudy remembered Clay asking his younger brother to throw rocks at him. However many rocks Rudy threw, he could never hit Clay. Even then Clay had some of the skills that would serve him so well in the ring, running left and right at speed, ducking, dodging, and weaving out of the way.

Odessa was a Baptist and Cash, as Clay Sr was known, was a Methodist but the boys always went to their mother's church. They never missed a morning of Sunday School and Clay remembered walking to church, knowing he looked handsome in his freshly ironed shirt and bow tie, and feeling proud of his pretty mother and handsome father. The Clays also instilled a sense of hard work in their boys. While Clay was at school, he worked at odd jobs to earn a few dollars a week and the boys used to accompany their father to work, where Cash taught them how to mix paint and lay out signs.

The Clays were a proud, contented family but not without problems. Cassius Clay Sr was arrested four times for reckless driving, twice for disorderly conduct and twice for assault. He had affairs and sometimes became violent when he was drunk. In fact, Odessa called the police three times when her husband turned nasty at home.

When Odessa Clay was taking her son's with her to church every Sunday, most churches, like this one, were segregated.

WHITE
WAITING ROOM
Postal Telegraph
HERE
2
3
4
5
CHATT

A DIVIDED CITY

Louisville was a quiet, peaceful city when Cassius Clay grew up in the 1950s and 1960s, but he became increasingly aware of the segregation around him. One of his first encounters with prejudice happened when he was very young, standing with his mother at a bus stop on a hot day. He was thirsty and when Odessa asked for a glass of water at a small diner nearby, the owner refused to help and closed the door in their faces.

Although he and Rudy didn't face real danger or violence in Louisville, as many people did in parts of the South, Clay was still shocked at being treated like a second-class citizen in the public realm, while being raised with pride and self-awareness at home. This was a time when laws known as Jim Crow Laws enforced segregation and made life difficult for African Americans. Louisville, like most cities, was a place where restaurants and swimming pools displayed signs that read 'Whites Only' and 'No Coloreds Allowed'. Black people had to go to separate schools, drink from separate water fountains and use separate restrooms. The boys never got into fights but white boys would call Clay and his brother 'nigger' and tell them to leave if they strayed into certain parts of town.

In spite of these challenges, Clay had a confidence and belief he was destined for great things from a young age. He remembers a time when, at about nine years old, he would wake up in the middle of the night and go outside to look at the stars and wait patiently for a message or a revelation from God. He never heard anything but never lost faith that a message would come.

In Clay's youth, segregation was a fact of life everywhere. There were separate waiting areas at bus stations (left) and separate entrances at theatres.

TURNING POINT

A message did come, but in the rather unlikely form of a local policeman named Joe Martin. In October 1954, when Cassius Clay was 12 years old, he and a friend cycled to the Louisville Home Show at Columbia Auditorium, mainly to sample the free food, popcorn and sweets on offer to visitors. When the boys had eaten their fill and were ready to leave, they discovered that Clay's bike had been stolen. Clay was furious and distraught – the bike was a new, red-and-white Schwinn that his parents had given him for Christmas. He was told to go and see a policeman, in the basement of the auditorium, who would fill out a police report for him.

Joe Martin was a Louisville cop who spent his spare time teaching boys to box for the city's recreation department in a gym, in the basement of the auditorium. When Clay burst in on Martin, the boy was crying and furious. He told Martin angrily that he was ready to search the whole state for whoever stole his bike and whip them soundly when he caught up with them. Martin asked if he knew how to fight. "No, but I'd fight them anyway," answered Clay. Martin replied, "Well, you better learn how to fight before you start challenging people that you're gonna whup," and gave Clay an application to join the gym, where boys could come and box every evening, Monday to Friday, from 6 p.m. to 8 p.m.

Call it chance or fate, this meeting was a turning point in Clay's life – everything changed when he entered the gym and started training. He began to learn the art and trade of boxing with a vengeance and would soon progress from a skinny kid with little talent into the greatest boxer that the world has ever known.

In this picture, taken at the gym in Louisville when he was just 12 years old, Clay looks young and vulnerable but his talent and training soon gave him the skills and confidence he needed to do more than strike the pose of a real boxer.

FROM AMATEUR TO OLYMPIAN

U.S.A.
U.S.A.

DETERMINATION AND DIET

A new boxing champion was born the first time Cassius Clay stepped into the gym. To make up for what he lacked in skill and experience, Clay had more than his share of determination and discipline. He began boxing with a vengeance. He spent all of his spare time training. He was the first one in the gym and the last to leave.

Clay trained six days a week and on school days he woke at four or five in the morning so that he could go running – what boxers call 'roadwork'. He was often seen racing city buses to school and was soon known by his peers as the kid who was obsessed with boxing. He took care about what he ate too, and over time, developed a special diet that included milk with two raw eggs in it for breakfast and a concoction of garlic and water that he drank throughout the day.

To go from skinny kid to Clay's strong boxing physique took relentless training and determination.

Joe Martin produced a popular local television show called 'Tomorrow's Champions' as part of the Columbia Gym's amateur programme. Boxing was important in Louisville and this Saturday afternoon show offered instant, local celebrity status to boxers. After just six weeks of training, Martin featured Clay on 'Tomorrow's Champions'. Thrilled at the prospect of being seen on television all over Kentucky, Clay trained even harder.

In his first ever televised bout, in 1954, he fought a local white boy named Ronny O'Keefe. Clay was only about 4 feet (1.2 m) tall and weighed just 89 pounds (40 kg), while O'Keefe was just a little older but bigger. The fight lasted three rounds of one minute each and Clay won by a split vote. From then on, Martin had him on the show each week. This was also the point at which Clay started bragging about being the greatest!

Clay's face shows the concentration and conviction he always had while training when he was young.

TOURNAMENTS AND TRAVEL

For the next few years, Clay continued to work and train hard, and to win the majority of the local fights. After 1958, he and other teenage boxers from the gym took part in boxing tournaments in different towns, including Indianapolis, Chicago and Toledo, staying in motels along the way. They were usually driven by Joe or his wife Christine Martin. Christine remembered young Clay as a very easy-going, polite boy who carried his Bible everywhere he went. She also recalled that in those days, the black kids were not allowed into restaurants, so she'd have to take their orders and get hamburgers for them to eat in the car.

By this time, Clay knew that he had a real talent for boxing and his dreams were going beyond earning enough to buy his parents a house and himself a fancy big car. Sometimes he would draw a picture of the back of a jacket with 'Cassius Clay, Golden Gloves Winner', or 'Cassius Clay, World Heavyweight Champ' written on it. Bob Surkein, an Amateur Athletic Union (AAU) referee and judge, recalled one tour in which Clay took all the sports sections from newspapers in a hotel shop and café so that he could cut out and keep all the pictures of himself.

Clay was also developing his own inimitable style. Instead of holding his hands up high to guard his head like most boxers, he held his gloves down low, and while most boxers stepped or ducked aside to avoid being hit, Clay leaned away from blows, risking throwing himself off balance. This unorthodox style worked for him because he had very fast reflexes and could throw a quick punch and dodge out of the way before other fighters could react. Soon, reporters, referees, and judges were talking about his presence and prodigious talent.

This is Clay in 1960 posing with Maxie Rosenbloom (left), Light Heavyweight Champion in 1932, and Solly Krieger (right), World Middleweight Champion in 1938.

Cassius Clay fighting against Gary Jawish during a Golden Gloves bout.

ON THE WAY TO THE OLYMPICS

Clay continued to train with Joe Martin and a more experienced coach named Fred Stoner. By the time he was 18 years old, he had fought a total of 105 amateur bouts, with 100 wins and just five losses. He won six Kentucky Golden Gloves Championships and two national Golden Gloves tournaments, in 1959 and 1960. He also won two national AAU titles.

This run of exciting wins had made Clay a local celebrity but he was yet to become really famous. This all changed when he was selected to represent the United States at the 1960 Olympic Games in Rome. Clay did well in the Olympic trials, but the trip to California for the trials was his first time on an aeroplane. It was such a rough flight that he declared he wouldn't fly again and that if he couldn't travel to Rome by train or boat, he wouldn't go at all. In the end he knew that if he wanted to be Heavyweight Champion of the world one day, he had to face his fears, so agreed to go but he bought a parachute from an army surplus store to wear on the flight!

When the Olympic team gathered in New York before the flight to Italy, Clay took the chance to try to meet one of his heroes, Sugar Ray Robinson. He waited all day outside Robinson's club but when the boxer finally appeared at ten o'clock and Clay stepped forward to talk to him, he remembers Robinson just patted him on the shoulder and said, "Later boy, I'm busy right now." Crushed, Clay vowed there and then that he would be different when he was a famous champion and that he would speak to, shake hands with or sign autographs for every fan he met.

At the Olympic Village, Clay stayed true to his vow and devoted attention not only to his training but also to meeting and greeting as many people as possible. He did as many interviews as he could and was often photographed. An unnamed team-mate said, "You would have thought he was running for mayor. He went around introducing himself and learning other people's names and swapping team lapel pins. If they'd had an election, he would have won in a walk." In fact, Clay even earned the nickname "the mayor of the Olympic Village".

Eighteen-year-old Cassius Clay raises his arm in victory after knocking out Gary Jawish in the 1960 Inter-city championships at Madison Square Garden.

Clay stands tall and proud wearing his gold medal for light heavyweight boxing in the centre of the winners' podium at the 1960 Olympic Games in Rome. On the right is Zbigniew Pietrzykowski of Poland who took silver. On the left are Giulio Saraudi of Italy and Anthony Madigan of Australia who took joint bronze.

TAKING GOLD

Clay's opening fight was against the Belgian Yvon Becot. It was stopped by the referee in the second round. He then beat the Russian Gennadiy Shatkov, who had won the middleweight gold medal at the 1956 Games in Melbourne in a unanimous points decision. In the semi-final Clay won again in a unanimous decision against Australian opponent Tony Madigan. In the final battle for the light-heavyweight gold medal, Clay fought Zbigniew "Ziggy" Pietrzykowski, an older, stronger and more experienced opponent. The first round didn't go well, with Clay taking some serious punches. The second went a little better, as he managed to throw four hard rights to Pietrzykowski's head, but he was still behind on points. Clay came alive in the third and final round. He was quick, coordinated and displayed perfect timing, with a flurry of both left and right punches, almost winning by a knockout blow, but in the end taking the match on points.

A spokesperson for the US Olympic Committee told The Associated Press that Clay "is putting on an amazing performance. In the ring he murders 'em with his fists. Outside the ring he kills them with kindness and his solid Americanism."

When Clay returned to Louisville after a three-week absence he received a hero's welcome. Crowds cheered as he passed through the streets in a 30-car motorcade escorted by the police. At a celebration at his school, he was met by Mayor Bruce Hoblitzell, cheerleaders and about 200 friends and fans. The mayor, on behalf of the Louisville Chamber of Commerce, told him that his gold medal was the key to the city. Clay read aloud what would be his first published poem: 'How Cassius Took Rome'.

When he was young, Clay loved to read about his victories in the newspapers.

HOW CASSIUS TOOK ROME

To make America the greatest is my goal,
So I beat the Russians, and I beat the Pole,
and for the USA won the Medal of Gold.
Italians said, "You're Greater than the
Cassius of Old."
We like your name, we like your game.
So make Rome your home if you will.
I said I appreciate your kind hospitality,
But the USA is my county still,
'Cause they're waiting to welcome me
in Louisville.

Clay was so proud of his medal that he even wore it to bed. He believed that the medal could change more than his career prospects. Sadly, it didn't. Before he had left the Olympic Village, a Russian reporter had asked him how it felt to win the gold medal for his country when there were still restaurants in the United States that wouldn't serve him. He replied that there were qualified people working on that problem and to him, the United States was the best country in the world. However, when Clay returned and he and a friend were refused service at a local whites-only restaurant while he was wearing the Olympic medal round his neck, he was furious. Legend has it that his response was to angrily toss the gold medal straight into the Ohio River.

AMPRO

ALI'S PROFESSIONAL CAREER

THE CONTRACT

After the Olympics, Cassius Clay was possibly the hottest property in boxing. His earning potential was huge. This attracted the attention of investors in Louisville who were prepared to pay big bucks to get a piece of the action.

The first interested party was Billy Reynolds, a Louisville metals millionaire. Clay never signed the contract Reynolds offered owing to his father. Reynolds stipulated that Joe Martin should play a role in Clay's professional career but Clay Sr. disliked cops in general, and Martin in particular.

A consortium of white businessmen turned boxing enthusiasts quickly came up with a better deal. The prime mover in the Louisville Sponsoring Group (LSG) was Colonel Bill Faversham, who was Vice President, sales, of the Kentucky distillers responsible for Jack Daniels and other popular drinks. Faversham and his friends, horse breeder Pat Calhoun and tobacco magnate Bill Cutchins, reckoned on $25,000 to launch Clay professionally so they contacted some investor friends, asking, "How would you like to buy a piece of a prizefighter?" Pretty soon there were ten in the consortium, each putting in $2800.

On 26 October 1960, Clay signed the contract and became a professional boxer. His deal included a $10,000 bonus, a minimum annual salary of $4,000 for two years and $6,000 for four years. Everything Clay earned, in the ring or otherwise, was to be split 50–50 with the syndicate, who paid all expenses, from his trainer's salary to housing rent.

US boxing promoter and prime mover in the Louisville Sponsoring Group (LSG) Bill Faversham is shown here speaking with Clay in 1963.

Clay celebrated the contract with a splurge: a pink Cadillac. He was soon cruising the streets of Louisville showing it off. In the following years the LSG became very rich from Clay's fighting, but also had to pay out a lot on anything from first class flights to the legal fees that kept Clay out of jail after speeding in the Cadillac.

Clay celebrated signing his first professional contract by buying a new Cadillac.

THE FIRST PRO BOUT

The LSG's official line was, "We are behind Cassius Clay to improve the breed of boxing, to do something nice for a deserving, well-behaved Louisville boy". They said they stepped in to make sure Clay was not prey to contracts with underworld mobsters. This was the case with the Heavyweight World Champion of the day: Sonny Liston. But the truth was that they knew Clay could make them richer. This was not just through their cut of his winnings in the ring, but also from sales amongst black boxing enthusiasts of the whisky and cigarettes they made and could advertise at Clay's fights.

Just three days after signing his contract, Clay fought his first professional bout. It had been organised over the preceding weeks by the LSG. Clay was to go up against one Tunney Hunsacker. Hunsacker was the 30-year-old chief of police of the little town of Fayetteville in West Virginia. Clay arrived at the Freedom Hall fight venue at the Louisville fairgrounds in his Cadillac. Hunsacker later recalled being 'pretty impressed' by the 'brassy young boy' and his entourage of supporters.

The police chief was a seasoned fighter who had fought more than 30 bouts. He soon realised that he was, "too old to be fighting an 18-year-old fella", once he got in the ring, even though he gave Clay, "some good chops to the stomach in the second and third rounds", that allegedly almost made the youngster bring up his hamburger dinner. However, Clay was too big and fast for Hunsacker, and had a trickily varied repertoire of punches. The six-round fight ended with a unanimous points decision for Clay and Hunsacker's eyes swollen shut. Clay was far from the finished article, but still gave the LSG cause for celebration that their investment was already paying dividends.

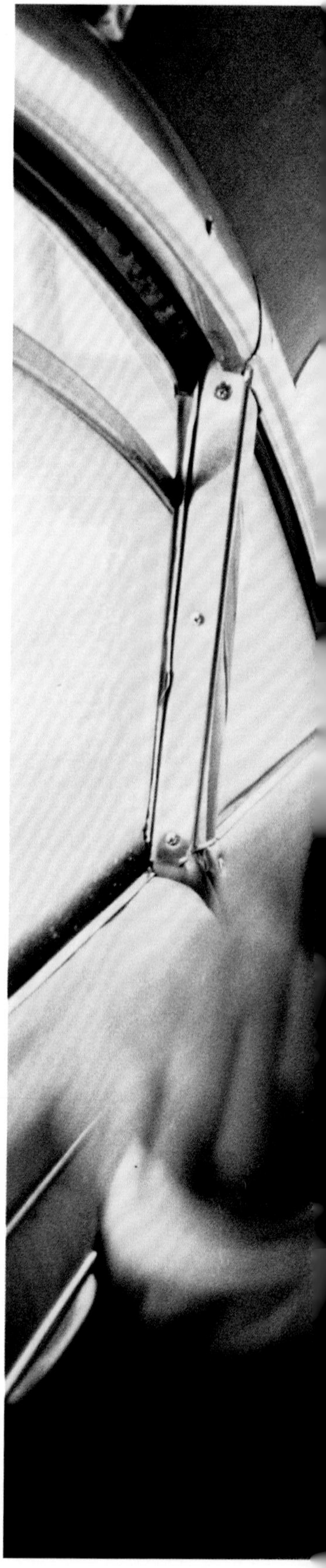

Clay's first professional bout against Hunsacker's was just the first on his road to success. At this point Cassius Clay knew he was going places.

Trainer Angelo Dundee was Clay's (Ali's) trainer from 1960 until the boxer retired.

A NEW TRAINER

In December 1960, the LSG syndicate made a move to back up their investment in Cassius Clay. They hired him a new trainer: Angelo Dundee. Dundee, based in Miami, had a great pedigree. He had trained 1955 World Welterweight Champion Carmen Basilio, and worked with title hopeful Willie Pastrano. Clay knew of Dundee because three years earlier, the 15-year-old boxer had stalked Dundee to a Louisville hotel, blagged a brief meet, and then quizzed Dundee for hours about all aspects of the boxing art.

Dundee quickly appreciated Clay's raw talents. The boxer was unusual in combining heavyweight power with the speed typical of the lighter divisions. Clay produced stinging jabs, usually to the head, that his friend and doctor Ferdie Pacheco called 'snake-licking'. But Dundee saw the faults, too. Clay often held his guard low and back-pedalled to evade punches. This could leave him off-balance or out of range for punching back, even with his long reach.

Dundee got to work. He further developed Clay's movement and balance. This was aided by sparring with Pastrano who was widely admired for his fleeting footwork. Dundee did not try to get rid of all the rough corners on his protégé. He once said, "Training fighters is like trying to catch fish," meaning that you have to go with what is already there.

The pair formed a close bond. Dundee was to remain as Clay's trainer through the coming years. His extraordinary abilities at training champions were sought by many other fighters, too. These included George Foreman, who in 1994, became the oldest Heavyweight Champion in history at the age of 45, and Sugar Ray Leonard who became World Champion in five different weight divisions.

Angelo Dundee was a brilliant motivator and was with Clay for virtually his entire career.

BOXER FOCUS: WILLIE PASTRANO

Wilfred Raleigh Pastrano was a pudgy child known as 'fatmeat' from the French Quarter in New Orleans. He took on a bully who was smacking him after his father, Frank, gave him the ultimatum: fight back or get a licking from me. Willie decided to take up boxing to lose weight at the suggestion of his friend Ralph Dupas. He went to the gym at night when there were fewer people around.

Pastrano lied about his age to fight his first professional bout when he was 15 years old and still at school. He was fined and had to remain amateur until he was 18. He started to spend summers in Miami at the training gym of Angelo Dundee, along with Dupas, who was a junior boxing champion. After high school, Pastrano moved to Miami where he further developed his fast hands and feet, and technical skills. In the early 1960s, Pastrano started to work with Dundee's new recruit, Cassius Clay.

Pastrano fought at heavyweight in the early professional years but with Sonny Liston rising to prominence, dropped down a division. In 1963, Pastrano's career had its high point. He won the Light Heavyweight World Championship, on a narrow points decision, against the overwhelming favourite Harold Johnson in Las Vegas. He only got the fight because other boxers had backed out. Pastrano defended the title twice, with unexpectedly hard hitting, before losing to José Torres in New York in 1965. This was when he retired. Pastrano by then was using drugs and had little money left. After working as nightclub bouncer and casino greeter, he eventually escaped the mean streets of Miami. He ran a municipal gym back in New Orleans where he trained many young fighters.

US heavyweight boxer Willie Pastrano training in 1958.

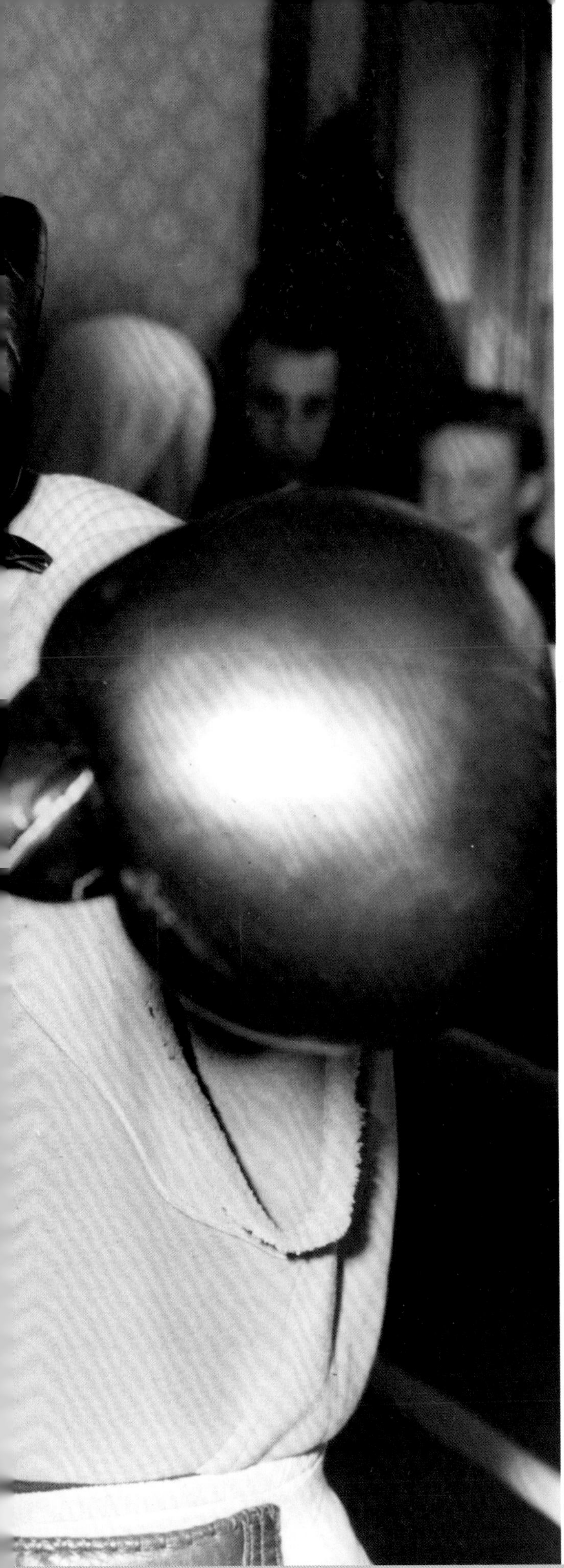

Pastrano held the World Light Heavyweight crown from 1963 until 1965.

STATISTICS

BORN	New Orleans (LA), November 1935
DIED	New Orleans (LA), December 1997
TURNED PROFESSIONAL	1950
NUMBER OF PRO BOUTS	84
WINS-LOSSES-DRAWS	63-13-8
NUMBER OF KNOCKOUTS	14
RETIRED	1965

Clay showing why he earned the nickname 'The Louisville Lip' at a press conference after he signed to fight Sonny Liston in 1963.

THE LOUISVILLE LIP

In the early 1960s, Cassius Clay was morphing into the boxing personality that the world came to know. At this time across the United States, the Civil Rights Movement was hitting its stride. There was pressure from black people to remain quiet and modest, aware that the opposite traits might offend some whites and derail the movement for race equality. Clay was a proud, loud, arrogant black man, happy to tell anyone who was listening about his boxing gifts. He also knew what he said – the boasts and the taunts – could impact his opponents, which is why Angelo Dundee called him 'The Louisville Lip'. The next step was to hone his public persona.

A seminal figure in this was the professional wrestler, George Wagner, who in his late 20s was transformed from a jobbing wrestler into the personality Gorgeous George. He became one of the first wrestling stars of the early days of colour television. Gorgeous George looked dramatic with long, curled blonde hair and sparkly robes. He entered the ring with special entrance music and valets threw roses and sprayed perfume into the crowd. He bad-mouthed his opponents and boasted at his triumphs. Crowds cheered or booed him.

Clay went to see Gorgeous George in Las Vegas in 1961 and was star-struck with his persona. And so he mimicked the wrestler's swagger, without the costumes and perfume. He proclaimed phrases such as, "To beat me, you have to be greater than great," and, "I will be the youngest champion in history". Some older boxers, such as Joe Louis, cautioned Clay; some people hated his self-praise, but as his fights and victories notched up, it was becoming clear that Clay did have something to shout about.

Henry Cooper jokingly looks at Clay's scales during the weigh-in before their fight at the Arsenal Stadium, London, in 1966.

SPREADING REPUTATION

Between his professional debut in 1960 until early 1963, Cassius Clay fought 18 different opponents and he won each fight: 14 by knock-out or technical knock-out. He fought across the United States, from Miami and New York to Las Vegas and Los Angeles. His reputation was growing fast and boxing was more popular than ever before, buoyed by increasing television audiences and the clamour for tickets to live boxing bouts.

Clay occasionally faced adversity in the boxing ring. In February 1962, he faced Sonny Banks in his 11th professional bout. This was the first time that Clay was ever knocked over. Near the start of the bout, Banks threw a left hook to the jaw that sent Clay flying but he got straight up. Angelo Dundee saw then that Clay could not only take punches, but also come back stronger. "That's when I knew I had a guy with greatness. It was remarkable how he survived that one punch. God he was exciting." Clay went on to win inside four rounds.

Clay devised a game with Dundee around this time. He started to predict the outcome of fights – how many rounds it would last. A good example of this is his fight against Archie Moore later in 1962. Moore was an old professional champion who had briefly trained Clay after the Olympics, but Clay did not like his authoritarian style. He correctly predicted a fourth-round knock-out, chanting, '"Archie Moore... Must fall in four."

Cassius Clay reached an even wider audience by travelling to London in 1963 for his 19th fight and first overseas professional bout. He took on British Heavyweight Champion Henry Cooper in front of 55,000 people and, again, correctly predicted a win in five. But Clay was lucky – he was floored by a phenomenal left from Cooper. Clay struggled to get up, but was saved by the bell marking the end of the round.

Henry Cooper and Clay in action in 1966.

BOXER FOCUS: SIR HENRY COOPER

Henry Cooper and his twin George were born in London and grew up during the Blitz years of the Second World War when the city was under attack. The boys came from a boxing lineage. Their father was a good amateur boxer in the Royal Artillery, and their horse trader grandfather was a bare-knuckle fighter who could fight 20 rounds. Henry and George joined Eltham Boxing Club and moved through the amateur ranks in England. Cooper won 73 of 84 contests, including the Amateur Light Heavyweight Championship in 1952.

Cooper became a dominant force in British professional boxing. In 1959, he won both the British and Commonwealth heavyweight titles. Back then he was still living at home, sharing a bedroom with George. He moved out only in 1960 when he got married. In the mid-60s Cooper was becoming internationally known for his crushing left hook – his left fist was popularly known as 'enery's hammer'. Buoyed by his close loss to Clay in 1963, Cooper challenged for the world title in a rematch against Muhammad Ali in 1966. History repeated itself as Cooper lost again after swelling and persistent bleeding above the left eye where the skin was thin – his jagged brow did him no boxing favours.

Cooper remained British champion until his narrow defeat to Joe Bugner in 1971. He became a national celebrity following release of a popular autobiography, appearances on BBC's *A Question of Sport*, television advertising for Brut aftershave and flu jabs, and his dedication to charitable work. His fundraising bought 100 coaches enabling sick or disabled children to go on holiday. Henry Cooper was knighted in 2000.

British boxer Henry Cooper at a function with his old rival Muhammad Ali in 1984.

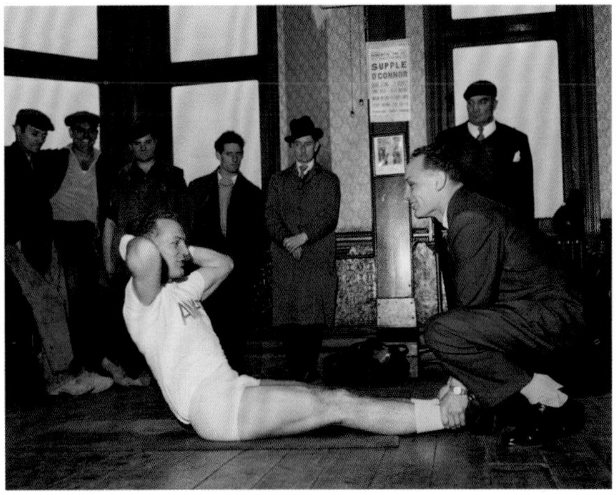

Henry Cooper and his brother George during a training session in 1958. Henry was preparing for a Commonwealth heavyweight title fight against Brian London.

STATISTICS

BORN	London, May 1934
DIED	London, May 2011
TURNED PROFESSIONAL	1954
NUMBER OF PRO BOUTS	55
WINS-LOSSES-DRAWS	40-14-1
NUMBER OF KNOCKOUTS	27
RETIRED	1971

WORLD CHAMPION

Cassius Clay talks up his chances of beating Sonny Liston at a press call before the fight in 1964.

GETTING A SHOT

In early 1964, boxing in the United States was massive. It had far more press coverage than basketball, tennis and athletics were still amateur-only sports and it was the quiet season for baseball and American football. Heavyweight was the most talked about boxing division. The two biggest stars in this division were the champion, Sonny Liston, and the young pretender, Cassius Clay.

The contrast between the two men fascinated the nation and the boxing world. Clay was handsome, eloquent and brilliant but his near defeat to Henry Cooper suggested he was an unfinished article. Liston, however, was a sullen and quiet, unstoppable force of nature.

Clay had had Liston in his sights for years and in 1964, thought he was ready. The boxers' handlers fixed a match for 25 February at Miami Convention Hall. In the run-up to the match, Clay trained hard in Miami, with the occasional break for press events including meeting the phenomenally popular Beatles, who were on tour. He also took time to plague Liston with taunts and boasts. At 3 a.m. outside Liston's rented Miami house, Clay parked a vehicle sign-written with 'Cassius Clay Enterprises' and shouted out that he was 'bear hunting' until the furious Liston ran out with a poker in his hand. At a press conference Clay read out a poem in which he imagined he'd punch Liston out of the ring:

"Who would have thought when they came to the fight,
That they'd witness a launching of a human satellite.
Yes the crowd did not dream when they put down their money
That they would see a total eclipse of the Sonny."

Clay noisily predicted he would knock out Liston in eight rounds. When reporters asked Liston how long Clay would last, he simply raised two fingers. The public antipathy between the men only pumped up expectations for the fight.

BOXER FOCUS: SONNY LISTON

Charles 'Sonny' Liston was the youngest of 25 children. His abusive and alcoholic father, Tobe, worked in cotton fields near Little Rock, Arkansas, and forced Sonny and his other children into hard labour, too. Sonny and his mother Helen escaped Tobe's domination when she started a new life working in St. Louis.

Sonny was 6 feet (1.82 m), 200 pounds (90 kg), incredibly strong and illiterate. Out of place amongst city kids, he fell into gang fighting and armed robbery. In 1950, he was jailed for five years at Missouri State Penitentiary Life. In jail a priest encouraged him to take up boxing and Liston soon rose to jail heavyweight champion.

Liston was paroled in 1952 by boxing handlers with alleged links to organised crime. He shot through the amateur ranks and turned professional in 1953. He became known as 'The Bear' owing to his frightening power, 15-inch (38-cm) circumference fists, and record of short bouts with knockouts. After a stretch in the St. Louis Workhouse for assault in 1956, Liston relocated to Philadelphia, where his professional contract was bought out by Mafia bosses. Liston defeated the popular fighter Floyd Patterson to take the World Heavyweight Championship in 1962. After two defeats to Clay in 1964/5, he carried on boxing for a further five years.

Sonny Liston was found dead at his Las Vegas home on 5 January 1971. Many suspected a mob execution, probably by enforced overdose, as there were traces of heroine in Liston's blood and needle marks on his arm and Liston had always been afraid of needles. It is alleged that he signed his own death warrant by refusing to throw a fight.

Sonny Liston in 1958.

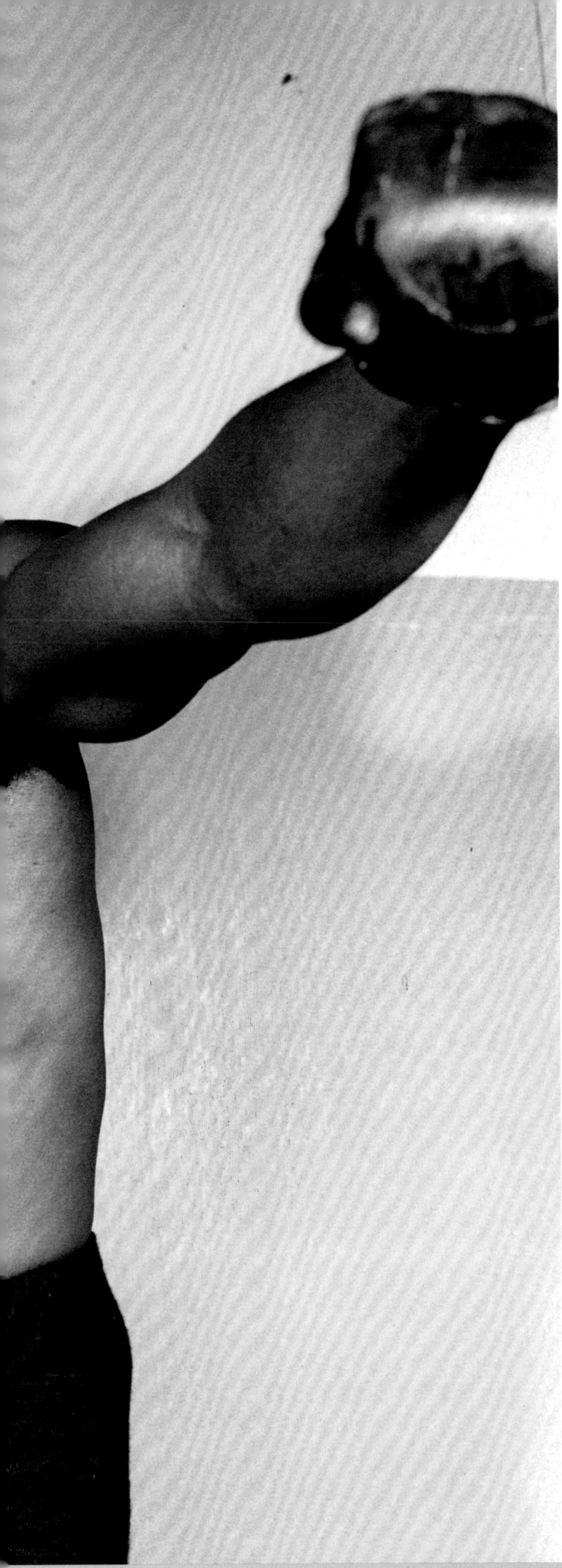

Sonny Liston and Floyd Patterson (left), during a championship fight won by Liston in just one and a half minutes.

STATISTICS

BORN	St. Francis County, May 1932 (uncertain)
DIED	Las Vegas (NV), December 1970
TURNED PROFESSIONAL	1953
NUMBER OF PRO BOUTS	54
WINS-LOSSES-DRAWS	50-4-0
NUMBER OF KNOCKOUTS	39
RETIRED	1970

8-1 CHANCE

It was not looking good for Cassius Clay. The bookmakers were giving odds of 8-1 for a Liston whitewash. In the days before the fight just 3 out of 46 boxing writers predicted a Clay victory. At the weigh-in on fight day Clay was pumped up more than anyone could remember. He screamed at Liston, "Someone's going to die at ringside tonight!"

The Convention Hall was only half full owing to limited hopes for a long fight, but many ex-world champions, including Sugar Ray Robinson, Willie Pastrano, Rocky Marciano and Joe Louis, were there to see how Clay would fare, and maybe even witness an upset.

Onlookers saw how Clay was taller than Liston and refused to be stared down by 'The Bear'. The fighters started warily with Cassius evading jabs and wild punches from Liston, but then Clay threw a rapid combination of punches. Liston staggered, outboxed. The champion fought back in the second round, but in the third he was hurting as Clay ramped up the head blows. Liston was cut on the cheekbone and reeling.

In the fourth round, Liston landed his best punch and Clay started blinking, rubbing his face, ducking and backpedalling. At the bell, he told Angelo Dundee he couldn't see properly, and Dundee demanded he continue but stay out of the way of Liston. Later it was alleged that Liston had put stinging liniment on his gloves to slow his opponent. Clay's eyes were wide open by the start round six and he laid into Liston's face, punch after punch. Liston appeared dazed as he slumped in his chair at the bell. He didn't come out for round seven.

There was pandemonium in the ring. Clay bounded around, arms raised, shouting, "eat your words" at the assembled press. Cassius Clay was the new Heavyweight World Champion.

Cassius Clay's expression says it all in the moments after he beat Sonny Liston and became Heavyweight Champion of the World.

Cassius Clay shows off his World Champion belt.

THE GREATEST

"I don't have a mark on my face. I upset Sonny Liston. I just turned 22. I must be the greatest. I shook up the world! I shook up the world! I shook up the world! I shook up the world!" Cassius Clay

Cassius Clay ponders his stratospheric rise in US and world sport, and boxing opportunities to come. What would happen to top his achievements in the early 1960s?

Cassius Clay's victory was one of the biggest upsets in boxing history. He had talked the talk and walked the walk. But he had had severe doubts he could win. Clay's doctor, Ferdie Pacheco, later said, "This was the only time I saw him nervous... he had no idea if he could do what he had been saying he could do."

Clay put his victory down to being too fast for Liston. But there were other factors. One was complacency on Liston's part. In the three-and-a-half years preceding their bout, Liston had been in the ring for just more than 13 minutes! That was because he kept beating opponents quickly. Another was an alleged injury. Straight after he quit on the night, he told a reporter that his left shoulder "feels like it's broke". He later claimed he could not punch properly after the flurry in the initial round owing to a strained muscle, possibly resulting from extravagant punching in round one, or a training injury. Many thought the claims were just sour grapes. After all, Liston could fight through pain – his only defeat as a professional before the Cassius Clay fight had been against Marty Marshall, when he had suffered a broken jaw and carried on fighting until the end.

Suddenly Clay's claims in interviews, at the ringside or even on later records and in books, to being 'The Greatest', were no longer sounding like hollow boasts. Everyone witnessing his performance now knew that he was the real deal. His boasts still irritated many, but their substance was undeniable.

Smok
Joe
MUHAMMAD
ALI

BECOMING MUHAMMAD ALI

I'M FREE TO BE ME

Two days after his victory in the Liston fight, which had made Cassius Clay the youngest Heavyweight Champion in history, he made an important announcement. He told a press conference that he was a follower of the religion of Islam, and that among the reasons for his conversion from Christianity was the discrimination against black people in the United States and his refusal to support integration. By making this stand, Clay was telling the United States, "I don't have to be what you want me to be. I'm free to be me."

Clay had first stepped into a mosque in 1961 and later said it was the first time he felt truly spiritual. He liked what he heard and started to read the Islamic newspaper *Muhammad Speaks* and attend regular meetings. He was soon seriously considering becoming a Muslim. He was linked to an organisation known as the Nation of Islam and the teachings of one of their leaders called Elijah Muhammad, a man who preached powerful messages of emancipation and believed Islam was the only religion for black people and that Christianity was the religion of white people. This argument proved a powerful one to Clay, who had seen injustices all his life and faced discrimination every day.

Clay attended meetings in the temple and read and learned from the Quran – the only difference between him and other Muslims was that he didn't have the same duties to carry out because of his profession. Clay also introduced his brother Rudy to his mosque and to Islam, and although he had discovered Islam later than Clay, it was Rudy who converted first, changing his name to Rahaman Ali. Clay waited to make a public declaration of his faith because he feared he would not have been allowed to fight in the championship if people knew that he had converted to Islam.

Clay's victory against Liston gave him the confidence to pursue his beliefs.

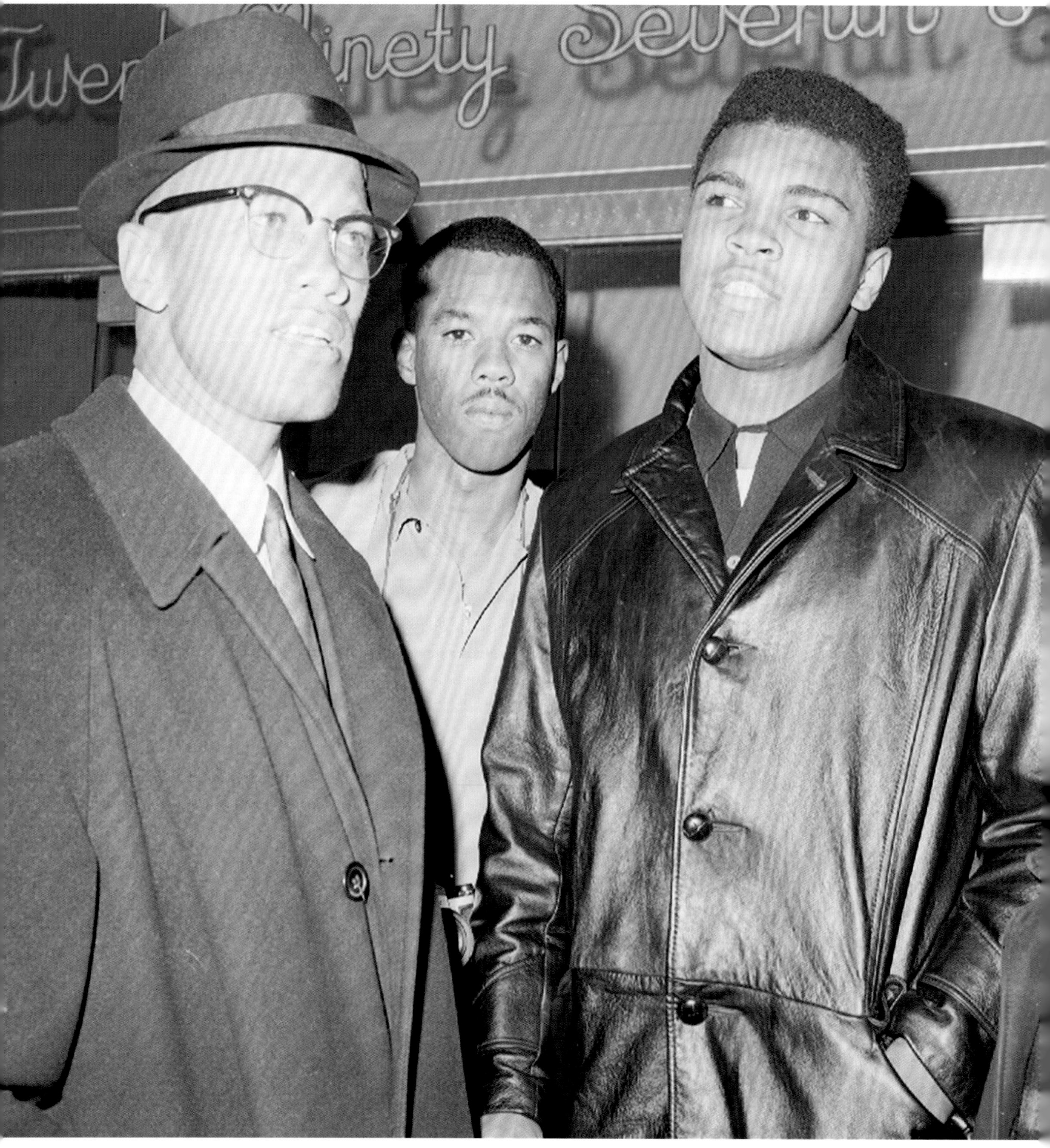

Cassius Clay with Malcolm X (left).

FROM CLAY TO ALI

Clay was also influenced by his friendship with Malcolm X, who he met in 1961 at a Nation of Islam meeting. Malcolm X supported Clay and stayed at the Miami training camp before the Liston fight. In March 1964, Malcolm X met Clay in New York and took him on a tour of the United Nations where they were photographed with African delegates. While at the UN, Clay signed his name Cassius X Clay and later that day, he rejected what he'd come to see as his slave name and accepted a new name, as given to him by Elijah Muhammad, Muhammad Ali. Muhammad meaning 'worthy of praise' and Ali the name of a great general and cousin of the Prophet Muhammad.

Many in the boxing establishment and the press did not respond well to Ali's change of religion and name. Some treated it as a fad he'd soon get over; many believed he was being used as an instrument of hate and refused to call him anything other than Cassius Clay. When Ali went to watch a fight at Madison Square Garden in March, the President refused to use the name Muhammad Ali when introducing well-known boxers in the audience. When Ali walked out by way of protest, the audience booed.

In May 1964, to get some respite from these tensions and the glare of the press, Ali began a month-long tour of Africa, visiting Ghana, Nigeria and Egypt. He met Egyptian President Gamal Abdel Nasser and Ghanaian President Kwame Nkrumah and was greeted by cheering crowds wherever he went, repeatedly calling out, "Who's the Greatest?" for the response, "You are!" In a speech during his trip, he announced, "In America everything is white. I am glad to be here among my own people."

Residents of Ghana cheer for Muhammad Ali during his visit there in 1964.

Muhammad Ali sits attentively listening to Elijah Muhammad giving a speech at a Nation of Islam meeting in 1964.

TIME OF TENSIONS

Muhammad Ali returned from Africa to rising tensions in the Nation of Islam. A rift between Elijah Muhammad and Malcolm X had become publicly apparent when Malcolm X said President Kennedy's assassination in 1963 had been, "chickens coming home to roost", which went against the Nation's stance of no comment on the popular leader's death.

In early 1964, Malcolm X had made a pilgrimage to Mecca where he witnessed people of different colours worshipping together, making him question the Nation's core belief of Islam being a black religion. In spite of Malcolm's attempts to persuade him otherwise, Ali chose to side with Elijah.

In Africa, Ali snubbed Malcolm, and after Malcolm X was assassinated in early 1965, Ali was not there at the funeral. In later life Ali expressed his regret at his treatment of his former close friend.

Ali also faced tension from his parents. His mother was convinced her son would not have converted if the LSG had not sent him far from home to Miami. His father was concerned that the Nation was just after Ali's money. Elijah had asked his son, Herbert, to help with Ali's business dealings with LSG and other white sponsors. Herbert became Ali's personal manager and also spiritual advisor, and was a constant presence in the Ali entourage. Ali's parents were concerned that Herbert would ruin Ali's professional life. They were also aware of their diminishing influence over Ali. A prime motive in Ali's life was now that of pleasing Elijah and, in many ways, the Nation had become his close family.

Ali also faced the threat of physical danger in the world outside the ring as a result of being in the Nation of Islam. In the days following Malcolm X's funeral, there was a mysterious fire in Ali's apartment, which was unoccupied at the time, and the Nation's headquarters were firebombed.

People queued to pay their respects at the funeral of Malcolm X. Malcolm X was a divisive figure in the United States and in the Nation of Islam. Although he had uncompromising beliefs, his powerful speeches attracted large crowds of people. He played an important role in Ali's life by introducing him to Islam.

Ali, wearing a white towelling robe, wades through members of the press to reach the ring for his rematch with Sonny Liston in St. Dominic's Arena, Lewiston, Maine, on 25 May 1965.

LISTON REMATCH

In early 1965, Ali was focussing all his energy on his rematch with Sonny Liston. The fight had been postponed from November 1964 in Boston when, three days before the fight, Ali was rushed to hospital for surgery on a swelling hernia. Liston, who after training was in better condition than the first match, had little sympathy for Ali, saying the hernia had been caused by, "all that hollering".

The fight was rescheduled for 25 May 1965, this time in Lewiston, Maine, rather than Boston, owing to concern about attacks by anti-Nation of Islam factions. The crowd in Lewiston was just a few thousand strong, but the fight was shown in movie theatres and on television nationwide. Liston was 9-5 favourite and people expected a closer, longer encounter. Ali predicted victory in the ninth.

Ali won in round one with his third punch, which became known as 'the phantom punch'. Ali had set his feet before throwing a fast, powerful right into Liston's jaw. Liston was up-ended onto the canvas. Ali stood over Liston shouting: "Get up and fight, sucker!" He was livid to be denied the chance to demonstrate he was champion by rights – Ali felt that Liston's claims of a bad shoulder had devalued his earlier victory. Liston did get up before the count had finished, but the referee called the fight a few seconds later.

There were allegations that the fight was fixed and that Liston took a fall so his mafia connections could make good betting money. It was rumoured that Liston was in poor shape having been taking heroin in the run-up to the rescheduled bout. Liston said that Ali standing over him at the count prevented him getting up. Just after the fight, Liston said of the phantom punch that he, 'saw it too late'.

Ali reacted angrily to Liston's first round defeat in 1965. He had won again but had also been denied the chance to prove his mastery in the ring.

A relaxed Floyd Patterson (left) sniggers at one of Ali's jibes at a press conference announcing their title bout in 1965.

BATTLE OF IDEALS

On 22 November 1965, Floyd Patterson challenged Ali for a championship fight. Patterson and Ali were old friends. Patterson as a past (1952) Olympic champion had mentored Ali at the 1960 Olympics. The pair had been in contact ever since. Patterson had been World Champion in 1956 and again in 1960, before losing badly to Liston in 1962, and was now aiming to regain the crown for the third time.

Ali typically decided that adding an edge of jibing before the bout would generate interest. Although friends, there was a fundamental difference in ideals of how to empower African Americans. Patterson was vocal in the Civil Rights Movement and wanted to end all segregation. The Nation of Islam supported segregation. For some, the bout pitted the two sides against each other. Frank Sinatra implored Patterson, his friend via civil rights rallies, to, "win the title back for America".

So, at press conferences, Ali called Patterson 'Uncle Tom' meaning he was subordinate to white people and 'rabbit' suggesting he was running scared of standing up for himself in society. He even showed up with a bag of carrots at Patterson's training camp. Patterson called Ali 'Cassius' to taunt him, although later he said he did it because a speech difficulty made it hard for him to say Muhammad.

The fight itself was a mockery. It was clear from the start to all, including Ali, that Patterson had an injured back – a slipped disc during training – and could not defend himself properly. Both fighters thought the bout would be stopped but the referee kept it going. The press viewed the match as an attempt by Ali to humiliate Patterson by keeping on punching and not delivering a knockout until round 12. But Ali did not want to hurt his friend unnecessarily. Patterson later said he had never felt such soft blows.

BOXER FOCUS: FLOYD PATTERSON

Floyd Patterson was the third of his parents' 11 children. He grew up in poor tenements in Brooklyn, New York. Floyd was a regular truant from school, stealing to try to help the family make ends meet. After several court appearances at age 11, he was sent to live in an upstate New York school for emotionally disturbed boys, for 18 months, where he learnt to read and write, and also took up boxing. Floyd turned amateur in 1951, and professional after winning Olympic heavyweight gold in 1952. For his first professional match, Floyd earned just $300.

Floyd was a leading professional when Rocky Marciano retired in 1956. He fought Archie Moore for the title in Chicago, in November that year. Floyd was sufficiently relaxed that he had a nap before the match, which he won on a technical knockout in the fifth, becoming the youngest heavyweight champion in history at that time. He defended his title twice before being beaten by the right hand – called the Hammer of Thor – of Swedish fighter Ingemar Johansson in 1959. Floyd regained his belt the next year but in 1962, was knocked out in round one by Sonny Liston. Floyd was so embarrassed that he left the venue afterwards wearing a false beard, moustache and dark glasses.

He failed to beat Liston again and Ali twice before retiring in 1972, after 20 years professional fighting. Patterson was a quiet, thoughtful man who became chairman of the New York State Athletic Commission and promoted boxing as a way out for children living in inner city ghettos. He suffered from Alzheimer's in later life to the point that he could not remember who he had fought for the title in 1956.

Boxer Floyd Patterson strikes a pose.

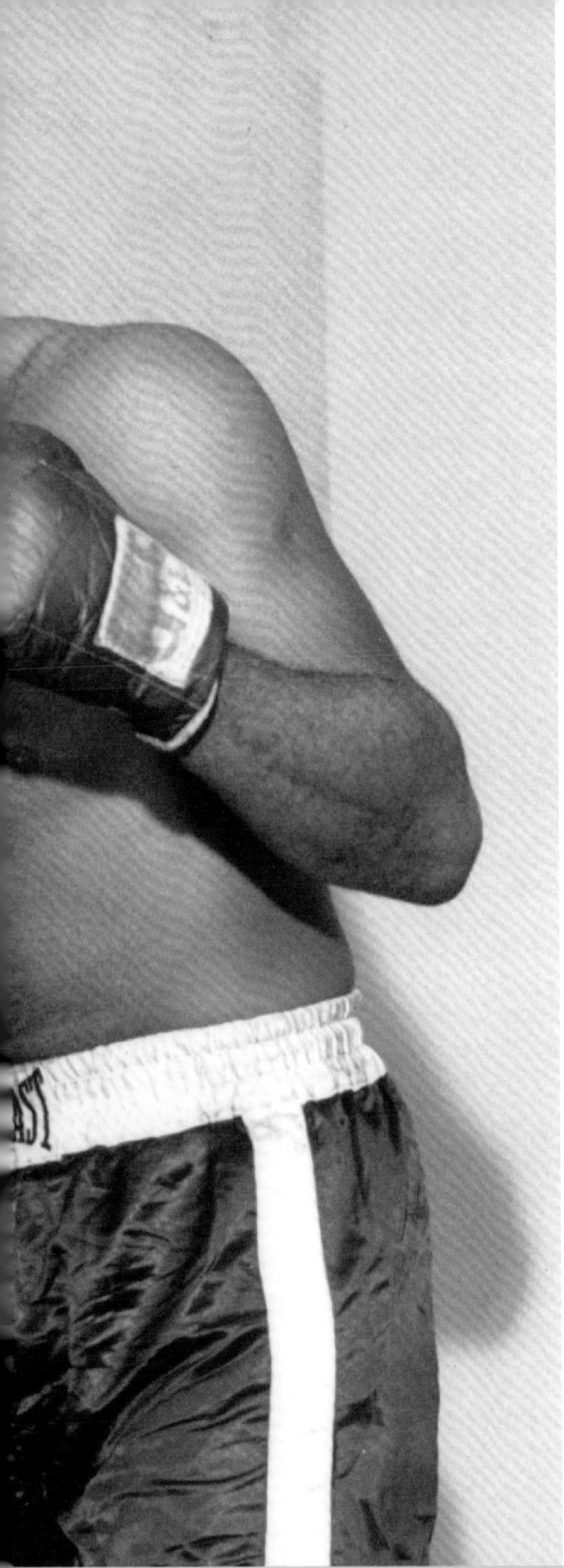

Patterson is declared victor. He retained his World Heavyweight title after a technical knockout in round 12 against Tommy Jackson in New York on 30 July 1957.

STATISTICS

BORN	Waco (TX), January 1935
DIED	New Paltz (NY), May 2006
TURNED PROFESSIONAL	1952
NUMBER OF PRO BOUTS	64
WINS-LOSSES-DRAWS	55-8-1
NUMBER OF KNOCKOUTS	40
RETIRED	1972

CALLED TO SERVE

In 1964, Ali had failed a mental aptitude test that would have qualified him to fight in the Vietnam War, a fact that caused him some embarrassment, especially when his less-than-impressive school records were publicised, too. By 1966, the Vietnam War was escalating and Ali was declared eligible and received his draft notice to join the US Army. He objected on the grounds of his religious beliefs and his response to the press: "Man, I ain't got no quarrel with them Vietcong," soon made front-page news. Many in the media and many ordinary US citizens, who at this time still supported the war, were vitriolic in their condemnation of his stand.

In Chicago, feelings ran so high that Ali's much-publicised fight with Ernie Terrell, scheduled for March, was cancelled and although promoters tried for venues in other cities, soon Terrell himself wanted no part in it either. An alternative opponent was found, Canadian heavyweight champion George Chuvalo, for a fight in Toronto, but there were calls for people to boycott this bout, too. The fight went ahead, and although Chuvalo was a tough nut to crack, Ali had more talent, and won 14 out of the 15 rounds.

After Chuvalo, Ali's promoters decided the best way to make money was to have him fight abroad. Three European bouts were scheduled. In May 1966, Ali fought and won a rematch against Henry Cooper. In August Ali was in England again and knocked out Brian London in three rounds. Then as undefeated Heavyweight Champion, he fought Karl Mildenberger in Frankfurt, Germany. Mildenberger put up a good fight, but Ali ended it in round 12 with a right hand that sent his already-bloodied opponent staggering against the ropes, prompting the referee to stop the fight.

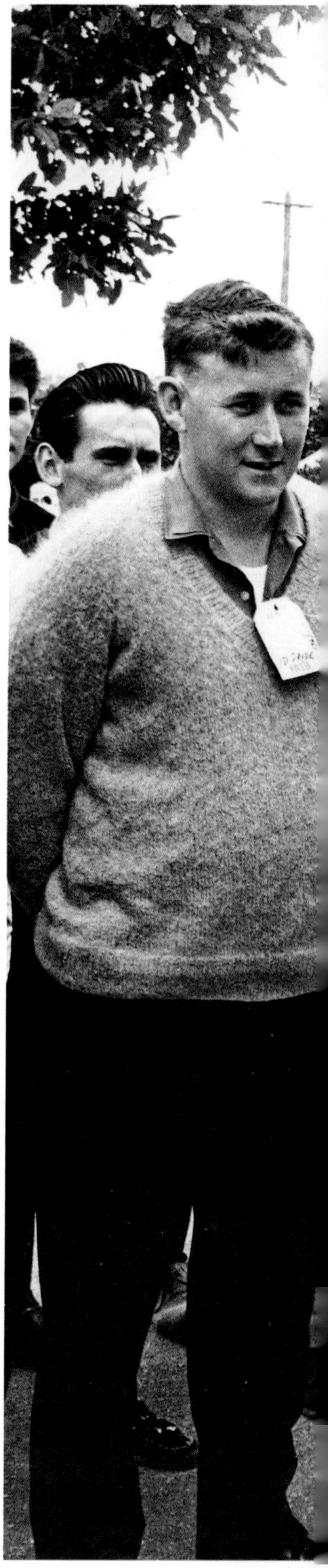

New conscripts group after being conscripted to fight in the Vietnam War. By the mid-1960s there was a major drive to draft men over the age of 18 in the United States and other countries, including Australia, to bolster ground troop numbers in the escalating conflict. Part of this was making changes to eligibility so fewer fit people were exempt from the draft.

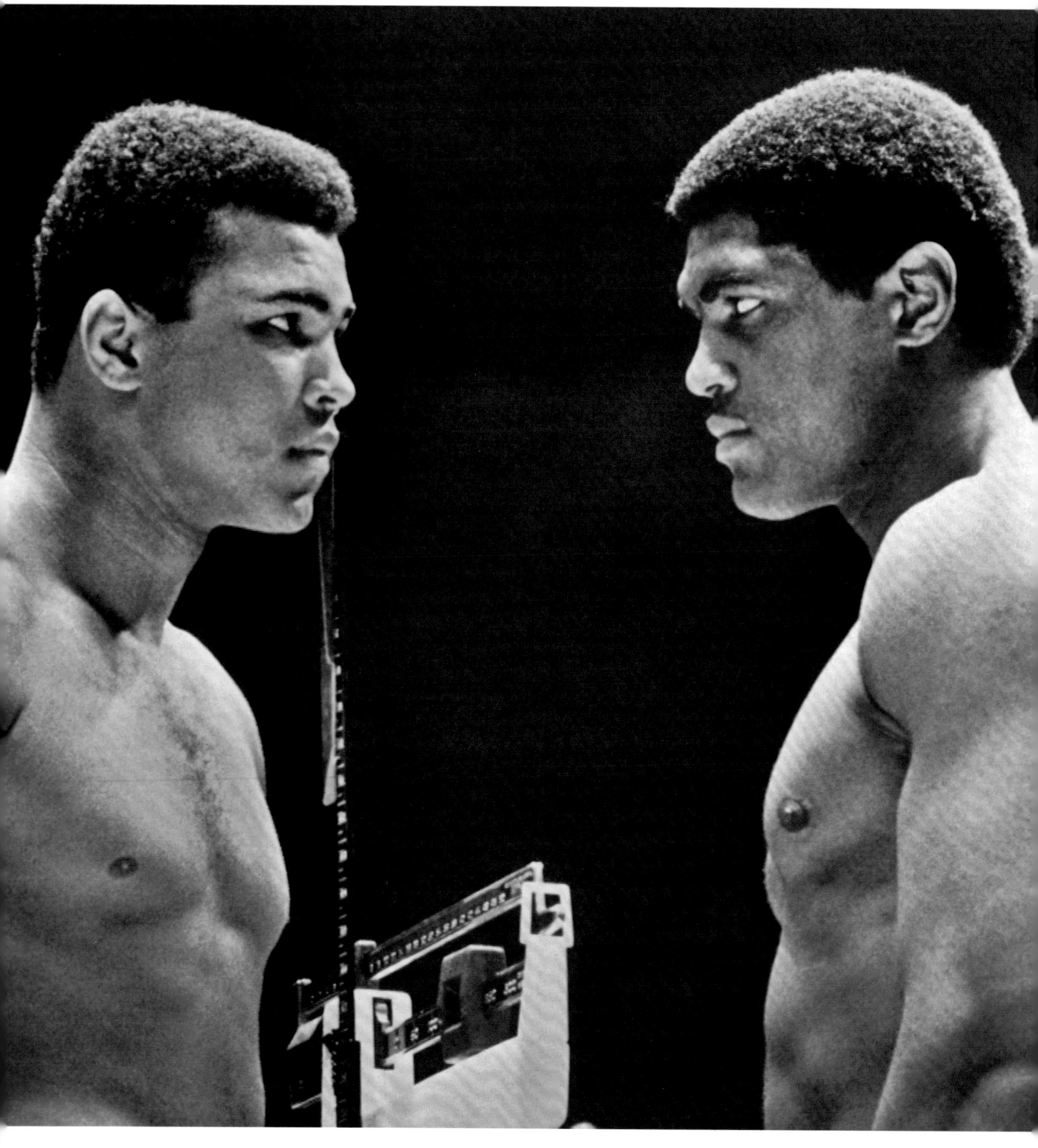

Ali eyeballs his challenger Ernie Terrell at the weigh-in before their championship bout in Houston, Texas, in 1967.

GRUDGE MATCH

There was no love lost between Ernie Terrell and Ali in the run-up to their bout in the Houston Astrodome on 6 February 1967. In a television interview the previous December, Ali read a poem, probably written by his friend and cornerman, Drew 'Bundini' Brown, about how Terrell, "will catch hell at the sound of the bell".

Terrell responded, repeatedly calling Ali 'Cassius' to which Ali angrily asked why he could not call him by his chosen name. The two scuffled on camera. Two days before the fight, Ali announced that he wanted to 'torture' Terrell. Terrell later claimed: "I had no animosity. I understood it's a fight. What he say, all that don't count."

The fight was brutal. Terrell's defence of holding his hands high with his elbows together worked in the opening round. Ali could not hit Terrell's head and had to keep his distance from Terrell's arms. In round two, Terrell was cut under his eye. He later said it was the result of Ali intentionally poking his thumb in his eye. Round four was Terrell's best, with a right that sent Ali staggering against the ropes.

Round five, Ali had gauged Terrell's hitting radius and had started to move closer, close enough to make his rapid, hard punches count. Terrell grew gradually groggier with multiple head shots. In round seven Ali almost knocked him out with a violent right-left combination. In round eight Ali started to repeatedly taunt Terrell saying: "What's my name? What's my name," before hitting his head. By the 12th round, Dundee was telling Ali to "finish him" as his fighter was tiring, but the bout did not finish until the end of round 15.

Terrell's defence proved increasingly inadequate against Ali's speed and power as their fight progressed.

ARREST AND TRIAL

By March 1967, the issue of Ali's stand against the Vietnam War was coming to a head. He received an order to report for induction into the army on 11 April, which his lawyers had changed to 28 April so that he could fight Zora Folley on 22 March at Madison Square Garden. Ali knocked out Folley in the seventh round.

As 28 March approached, Ali became more vocal about his protest, saying: "Why should they ask me to put on a uniform and go 10,000 miles from home and drop bombs and bullets on brown people in Vietnam while so-called Negro people in Louisville are treated like dogs?" His stand made him a figure of hate for many people and even his supporters received death threats and had their car windows smashed. When the day finally came, Ali went through the morning's formalities and health checks, but when the time came for him to step forward, he refused. He was taken back into the room and given a second chance to take the oath, but he again refused. He then signed a statement to that effect.

Within an hour of Ali refusing the induction, the New York State Athletic Commission suspended his boxing licence. The rest of the boxing world soon followed suit, and Ali was stripped of his heavyweight title. His trial began on 19 June 1967. Ali argued he was entitled to exemption as an appointed minister of the Nation of Islam. However, exemptions from military service on religious grounds were allowed only for conscientious objectors who opposed war in any form, whereas when questioned, Ali acknowledged that he would take part in an Islamic holy war. He was convicted of refusing induction into the US Army and given the maximum sentence allowable – five years in jail and a fine of $10,000.

Ali holds up the cover of Nation of Islam newspaper. Muhammad Speaks referring to his trial to the watching media in 1967.

Ali appealed against his conviction and he was allowed to remain free, out on bail, while the appeal was processed. As he was banned from fighting in the United States and his passport was confiscated, he could not travel abroad to fight so he could not box to earn a living. It seemed that Ali was going to take his hardest hits outside, not inside, the ring. "He did not believe he would ever fight again," Ali's wife at the time, Belinda Ali, whom he married on 17 August 1967, said: "He wanted to, but he truly believed that he would never fight again."

Ali spent much of the next three-and-a-half years, while the courtroom fight ensued, going to Nation of Islam meetings and travelling the country giving talks at university campuses. He talked about the war in Vietnam, about integration and segregation, black pride, his views on being stripped of his title and denied the right to fight, and even on the financial hardships that brought him to make those lecture tours! He often got a mixed reception. In some places he was heckled and abused but even many of those who supported his anti-war and civil rights views, were shocked by some of his anti-gay, sexist and conservative statements.

These were tough times. Earnings from the lecture circuit didn't cover attorney fees for the ongoing appeal and Ali was still under constant government surveillance. In December 1968, he served ten days in jail for driving without a valid licence. Another blow came in April 1969. Elijah Muhammad had never agreed with boxing and after a statement Ali made to the press about wanting to go back into boxing if the money were right, Elijah suspended Ali from the Nation of Islam for a year.

Ali greets students while visiting St. John's University, New York, in May 1968. Ali's presence and messages of racial equality – by separation – transfixed student audiences across the United States during the years when he was banned from boxing.

HALL OF FAME SELECTIONS

Clay and Marciano battle it out in the ring.

FANTASY FIGHTING

Ali was running out of money and was desperate to find ways to earn outside the ring. In early 1969, he took a part in a documentary called *a.k.a. Cassius Clay* for $1000 a day to shoot interviews and recollections of his fights, which would be interspersed with archive footage.

Ali's next payday was more bizarre – a fantasy fight. A Miami advertising man named Murry Woroner had created a fantasy boxing tournament between the best heavyweights of all time in 1967. He input data about each fighter into a computer – such as speed, killer instinct, how prone to cuts – and then pitted each set of data against another in a "bout". Woroner presented this information as a blow-by-blow tournament radio show, which he successfully sold to many stations and gathered millions of listeners by 1968. Ali was outraged to hear that he had lost in the tournament to Jim Jeffries who he considered 'history's clumsiest' heavyweight, and sued Woroner for $1 million.

Woroner cleverly turned the situation around, offering to pay Ali $10,000 to film a fantasy fight supposedly controlled by computers against Rocky Marciano. The two champions met in a blacked-out gym in Miami and got on famously. Both were overweight and in poor fighting shape. Their job was to film 70 one-minute rounds of fake but realistic fighting, avoiding any hard or head punches – although Ali did accidentally knock off Rocky's toupee! They simulated cuts using ketchup as blood and filmed different knockout endings. No one knew who won until the film was presented in 1,000 movie theatres across the United States in 1970 – Rocky beat Ali. People in the audience booed, cried and yelled, not believing their eyes. Ali's supporters said he had humiliated himself: "They want your ass whipped in public... and not just by anybody, but by a real Great White Hope."

BOXER FOCUS: ROCKY MARCIANO

Rocco Francis Marchegiano's parents left Italy, during the depression era, for the United States in the hope of starting a new life. They settled in Brockton, MA, an area favoured by other Italian immigrants. Although his father found work in the city's shoe industry, the Marchegiano family lived in poverty. Rocco, who came to be known as Rocky Marciano, was one of six children and between casual jobs, was a keen amateur baseball player.

He was drafted to the US Army in 1943 and took up boxing to avoid duties such as washing dishes and cleaning latrines. He turned professional after leaving the military in 1947. Within two years he had knocked out 16 opponents and established his nickname: the Brockton Blockbuster. He was considered tough and rough but too short at under 6 foot (1.82 cm), too light at just 13 stone (82.5 kg), old (at 25) and lacking great technique. But he continued to improve and by 1951, faced up to his boxing hero, Joe Louis. Rocky knocked him out in round eight and then cried in Louis's dressing room afterwards in guilt.

In 1952, he took the World Heavyweight Championship in style by knocking Jersey Joe Walcott unconscious in round 13. Days afterwards, a triumphant Rocky rode in a convertible amongst crowds 10,000 strong – one of their own had become a sporting hero. Rocky defended his belt six times, coming close to defeat after a nose cut against Ezzard Charles. He retired in 1956, having never been beaten as a professional. For the following decade or so, Rocky made many personal appearances capitalising on his fame. He died in a private plane crash aged 46.

Rocky Marciano holds a victory pose after knocking out Jersey Joe Walcott to take the World Heavyweight Championship on 23 September 1952. Until that punch, Rocky had been trailing badly on points and an upset looked highly unlikely.

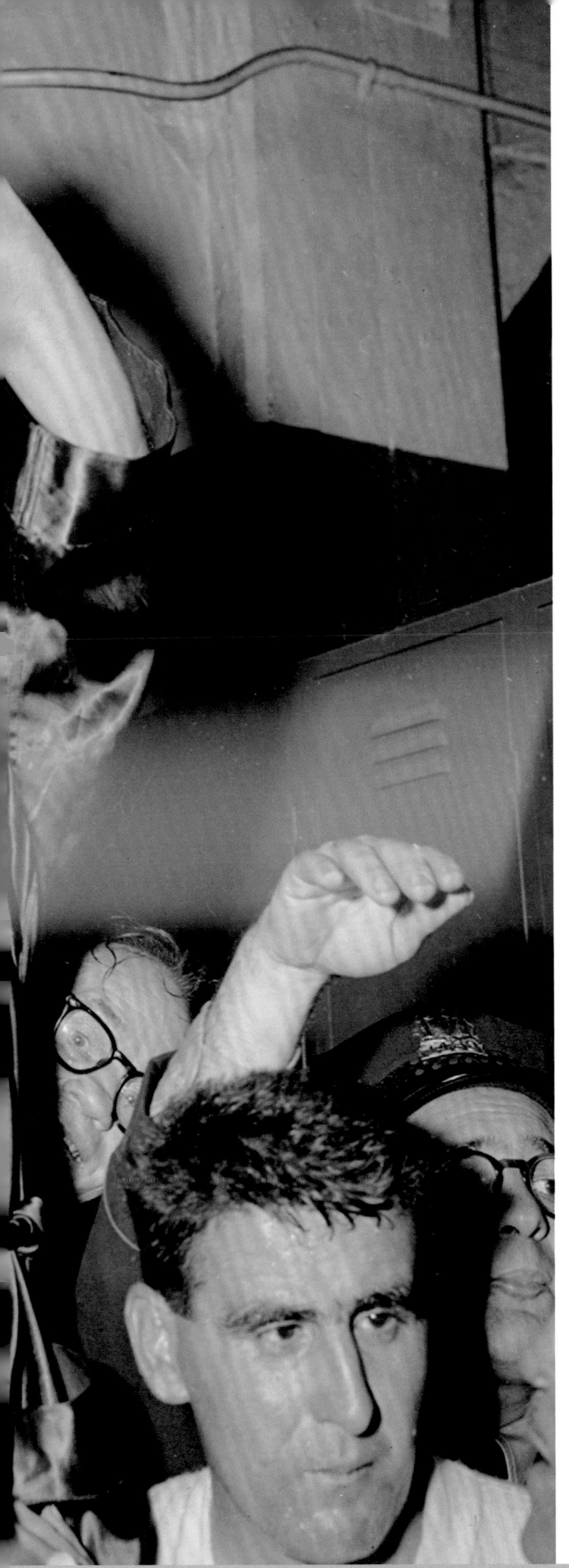

Rocky lands the right-hand piledriver that took out his childhood idol, Joe Louis, in their 1951 bout.

STATISTICS

BORN	Brockton (MA), September 1923
DIED	Des Moines (IA), August 1969
TURNED PROFESSIONAL	1947
NUMBER OF PRO BOUTS	49
WINS-LOSSES-DRAWS	49-0-0
NUMBER OF KNOCKOUTS	43
RETIRED	1956

Track and field athletes Tommie Smith (centre) and John Carlos (right), first and third place winners for the United States in the 200 metres, protest with the Black Power salute at Mexico City Olympics in 1968.

BLACK POWER

In 1969, Black Power was a mainstream issue in the United States. In in the previous year, millions of television spectators had witnessed two US athletes giving the Black Power salute from the Olympic medal podium in Mexico City. It symbolised that many African Americans believed white politicians were failing them and that they needed Black Power to help themselves.

The Black Panther Party was an extreme faction of the Black Power Movement. In this political party the members carried guns and believed that violence was justified in bringing about black justice. Many in the movement disagreed with their aggressive tactics and rhetoric, while endorsing their work in helping poor black communities.

In 1969, the musician, social activist and playwright Oscar Brown Jr opened and starred in his musical comedy about Black Power, *Buck White*. It was about the confusion and conflict in a black social organisation when a militant black leader, Buck White, addresses its members. The play did so well in California that producers decided to run it at the George Abbott Theatre on Broadway. The producers surprisingly cast Ali as Buck White in hope of drawing in crowds. Ali was 'dignified and impressive', singing songs such as 'We Came in Chains' with 'pleasant' voice. Unfortunately New York audiences were not taken and the musical ran for just seven performances. Theatre critic Kushauri Kupa said Ali had made a mockery of genuine protests by presenting a militant leader as a buffoon.

While on Broadway, Ali made a point of seeing the play *Great White Hope* about brilliant black heavyweight champion of the early 20th century, Jack Johnson. Johnson was a rebel in the Jim Crow era, dating white women, racing cars, openly displaying his wealth and bragging about his abilities. Ali said: "That's Me. You take out the white women, and that play is about me."

Ali poses outside the Broadway theatre showing a play about Jack Johnson, the revolutionary black boxer of the early 20th century. Ali saw deep parallels between his own outspoken stance and Johnson's views.

RETURN TO THE RING

abc
abc

Ali had to put in hard hours in the gym to get himself mentally and physically ready to fight at an elite level once more after his ban.

THE COMEBACK

In 1970, Ali's struggle to get back in the ring and win back the title of Heavyweight Champion of the World, now in the hands of the talented fighter Joe Frazier, heated up. Ali's lawyers and promoters worked hard to get permission for him to fight in different states but were denied time and again. Finally, a mayor in Atlanta, Georgia, was persuaded to allow Ali to fight against Jerry Quarry there, in spite of attempts by several members of Congress to stop it.

And so it was that on 26 October 1970, Ali fought again. It was a big moment for Ali and a stressful one: Quarry was strong and younger, a world-class opponent. The arena was filled with the rich and famous from the black community including Sidney Poitier, Bill Cosby and Jesse Jackson, and the crowd roared a delighted welcome to Ali as he entered the ring. Although Ali started well, he was slowing noticeably in rounds two and three, when he suddenly dealt Quarry a right punch that opened a huge, deep cut over the boxer's eye. This injury ended the fight and Ali was declared the winner but unsurprisingly, after three and a half years out of the ring, Ali's fitness was clearly not what it had once been.

While Ali's absence from the ring might not have been good for his training, the publicity that came from it certainly increased his fame and earning power. Ali was paid more for the Quarry fight than he had ever been paid before. While Ali's refusal to go to war and his exile had made him unpopular to begin with, by 1970, protests against the Vietnam War were growing and more people were thinking that perhaps Ali should not have been punished for his beliefs.

A deflated Jerry Quarry (left) looks past a triumphant Ali at the referee Tony Perez as he signals the end of Ali's comeback fight on 26 October 1970. Ali had won but he was not yet convincing championship material.

BOXER FOCUS: JOE FRAZIER

Joe Frazier was the seventh of 13 children of a sharecropper in South Carolina. He was a hard worker and strong – at age 12 Joe was making money filling sandbags – but to become fitter, he joined a gym. At the gym he discovered boxing and sailed through the amateur divisions until he faced Buster Mathis in the 1964 Olympic trials. Mathis beat him on points but then had to pull out of the event with a hand injury. Joe took his place, and the opportunity, winning heavyweight gold.

Joe turned professional in 1965 and sealed his reputation as a scrapper who could take heavy punches and still come through, with the help of a fearsome left hook, earning him the nickname 'Smokin' Joe'. In 1968, after Ali was banned, Joe fought Mathis again, this time for one of the several world championship titles being contested at that time. He took the New York State title on a technical knockout in round 11. He defended this title several times before beating Ali, who had returned after his ban and held one of the other heavyweight titles. With a famous left hook and unanimous points decision, Smokin' Joe became the undisputed Heavyweight Champion in 1970.

Smokin' Joe defended his title over the next two years but was then beaten by George Foreman – Olympic champion from 1968 – in Jamaica in 1973, Ali (twice) in 1974, and Foreman again in 1976. He then announced his retirement but five years later, returned to fight and draw a professional bout just once more. Joe went on to train fighters in his gym, but died after a long battle against cancer.

Joe Frazier in his mid-20s poses in a fighting stance in the ring with his trainer, Eddie Futch, looking on.

Frazier stands jubilant on 16 February 1970 after taking the World Heavyweight title against Jimmy Ellis on a technical knockout in New York.

STATISTICS

BORN	Beaufort (SC), January 1944
DIED	Philadelphia (PA), November 2011
TURNED PROFESSIONAL	1965
NUMBER OF PRO BOUTS	37
WINS-LOSSES-DRAWS	32-4-1
NUMBER OF KNOCKOUTS	27
RETIRED	1981

THE FIGHT OF THE CENTURY

After the Quarry fight, Ali won permission to fight in New York and on 7 December 1970, he took on Oscar Bonavena, winning in round 15 with a crowd-pleasing left hook. Now it was Ali's chance to win back his title by fighting Joe Frazier, who knew that he needed to defeat Ali before he would truly be accepted as the best in the world. Their meeting on 8 March 1971 at Madison Square Garden was billed as 'The Fight of the Century'. It was watched by 300 million people in 35 countries around the world. It made $1.3 million on the gate and guaranteed each fighter a fee of $2.5 million.

The promotional build-up was as tense as the fight itself. Ali infuriated Frazier by calling him 'Uncle Tom' and saying that anyone black who supported Frazier was an Uncle Tom, too. He even called Frazier ugly and dumb. Ali was clear afterwards that this was all pre-match hype, but Frazier never forgave him and this dislike formed a backdrop to this and their subsequent fights.

Ali was famous for nifty footwork and fast hands. Frazier's style was to stand firm and keep delivering hits. The two fought with skill and style and traded punches for an electrifying 15 rounds. In round six, Frazier pinned Ali to the ropes and battered him relentlessly, while in round nine it was Ali who dominated, hammering Frazier with right-left combinations. In round 11, Ali was nearly knocked to the floor by a Frazier hook but in rounds 12 and 13, Ali took the fight to Frazier. In round 15, Frazier knocked Ali to the floor and although Ali got up again, the fight was awarded to Frazier. Ali had lost his first professional fight since returning to the ring and he had officially lost the heavyweight title.

The moment when Ali's dream of becoming Heavyweight Champion once more was dashed by the power of Smokin' Joe Frazier at the end of the Fight of the Century.

Ali shows off the spangled robe given to him by Elvis Presley, before his fight against the Briton Joe Bugner in February 1973.

FREE TO FIGHT AGAIN

The loss in March 1971 was a huge blow to Ali and his supporters but after a rest, he resumed training. On 28 June, he received good news when the Supreme Court reversed his conviction. At last, Ali was free to fight anywhere again and his conscientious objection had been accepted.

While Ali waited for his next meeting with Frazier, he toured the world defeating opponents in Switzerland, Japan and Ireland as well as in the United States. In February 1973, he beat Joe Bugner in Las Vegas in an uninspiring bout that is mainly remembered for his jewel studded robe emblazoned with the words 'People's Choice' – a gift from Elvis Presley. Then in March 1973, a little known opponent, Ken Norton, surprised everybody by breaking Ali's jaw in the second round of a fight. Ali continued to fight on but finally lost in round 12. It took six months for Ali's jaw to heal. When the two fought again, it took 12 rounds for Ali to get even, winning a close but unanimous victory.

At last, Frazier agreed to a rematch with Ali and the date was set for 28 January 1974. By this time Frazier had lost the title to George Foreman, but Ali had a point to prove and Frazier hated Ali. In the build-up to the bout, the two traded bitter insults and were even involved in a brawl in a television studio. The event was another sell-out. On the night, the boxers kept up the brutal pace that had characterised their first meeting but this time, after 12 rounds, Ali was awarded a unanimous decision over Frazier. The two rivals had taunted each other throughout the bout and although Frazier had made Ali wait almost three years for a rematch, he was demanding another as soon as this one was over.

Ali was the People's Choice because he was a magnetic performer but many boxing experts were concerned that his best fighting days were over.

PROMOTING A LEGEND

Don King was a new boxing promoter on the block in 1972. King wanted to use Ali's legendary status to help him find fortune. After organising a hospital fundraiser featuring Ali in 1972, his ambitions stretched to putting on a heavyweight title bout between Ali and the incumbent champion, George Foreman. He promised the two fighters $5 million each but hit a brick wall in finding funding. Magically, a funder emerged: President Mobutu Sese Seko of recently independent Zaire would pay but only if the fight happened in his capital, Kinshasa. King met with Mobuto's advisers in Paris to forge a deal.

Don King and his friend Lloyd Price came up with King's up-combed hairstyle to give the promoter a distinctive look to accompany his distinctively flamboyant approach to boxing promotion.

Mobuto wanted to bring a major sporting event to Africa for the first time and thus demonstrate that he was a major player on the continent. African Americans including Ali and Foreman liked the symbolism of returning to their ancestral 'home' – Africa – for such a big fight.

Mobuto also had strong links with the United States. He had seized power in a military coup after killing the previous democratically elected leader, Patrice Lumumba, who Ali had met on his earlier African trip, with the clandestine aid of the CIA. The US government was concerned that Lumumba was giving too much power to 'communist' influences. Mobuto stabilised the country after years of turmoil, which earned him the friendship of several US presidents, but at a high cost. He amassed a massive personal fortune based on Zaire's mineral wealth while the vast majority of the population was living in poverty and brutally repressed by his state police and army. Tales abounded of Mobuto feeding opponents to crocodiles, and executing known criminals to maintain law and order in the months before the fight.

Ali poses for the press with fight posters advertising his Zaire Foreman fight in 1974.

In late September 1974, Ali was in intense training so he remained fighting fit while Foreman's eye injury healed.

ALI BOMAYE

When fight organisers arrived in Kinshasa in March 1974, they were shocked by what they found. The tiny runways at Kinshasa's airport were unsuitable for jumbo jets, there was a dirt track rather than road to the fight stadium and there was a lack of satellite technology so the fight could not be broadcast worldwide. However, when Ali and Foreman arrived in September, Mobuto had transformed the capital's infrastructure. Billboards along the airport road pronounced, "Black power is sought everywhere in the world. But it is realised in Zaire".

From meeting the locals to audiences with Mobuto, Ali felt at home in Zaire. Foreman was a more closed-off figure at this time, who stuck mostly with his entourage. Ali was 32 years old to Foreman's 25 years and the 3-1 underdog following Foreman's defeat of Frazier. Yet he talked up his chances of regaining his crown using speed and skill, repeating a famous phrase first coined by Bundini Brown:

'Float like a butterfly, sting like a bee
His hands can't hit what his eyes can't see'

Ali learnt a phrase, "Ako bomaye," meaning, "I will kill him", in Lingalla dialect. From that point on the crowds that came to see him chanted, "Ali bomaye", meaning, "Ali, kill him".

Eight days before the fight, Foreman's eye was badly cut by an accidental elbowing from a sparring partner. The fight was delayed for five weeks so it could heal, which was worrying for organisers as the impending rainy season risked making the open stadium event a washout. In the wait for the fight, Ali enjoyed spending time with musicians such as James Brown and Hugh Masakela at the Zaire '74 music festival, organised by Lloyd Price, a friend of King's, to take advantage of the fight's media attention.

Ali enjoys the noise from the adoring crowd lining his route, held in check by Mobuto's army, as he travelled around Kinshasa in late summer 1974.

Foreman tries in vain to scramble to his feet in round eight, still reeling from Ali's championship-winning punch combination. For all his power, Foreman had been outsmarted by Ali's tactics.

RUMBLE IN THE JUNGLE

In the early hours of 30 October, Ali and Foreman arrived at the Zaire national football stadium, the Stade du 20 Mai, in darkness. Ali, wearing a white satin robe trimmed with an African blanket, and his vast entourage arrived to the sounds of, "Ali bomaye" from the 60,000-strong crowd. In contrast, Foreman arrived in a simple red velvet robe. Mobuto was not even there. He watched the fight on television as he feared being assassinated in the open stadium.

Two national anthems, the Star Spangled Banner and Le Zarois, were played while the United States' and Zaire's flags were shown off in the ring. Ali said to Foreman: "You have heard of me since you were young... Now you must meet me, your Master." And then the fight began.

Ali landed two powerful head shots to signal his intent and then started to defend. He took whatever Foreman could throw at him. By the middle of round eight, Foreman started to tire after all that punching. Ali taunted him: "George, is that all you got?" then leapt at the opportunity when Foreman's guard was down. He summoned a fast, sledgehammer left-right combination that floored Foreman. Ali had predicted that Foreman would fall on his face from exhaustion in the tenth round, but his punches proved to be knockout blows. Foreman was counted out before he could stand up.

After a seven year gap, Ali was World Champion once more, only the second heavyweight after Floyd Patterson to regain a title. It was Foreman's first defeat in 41 bouts. Ali crowed: "I did it. I told you he was nothing but did you listen? ... I told you I was going to take all his shots. I told you he had no skill. I told you he didn't like to be punched."

Ali started fast against Foreman to remind his imposing opponent of his speed and power. But much of the bout was about a war of attrition.

ROPE-A-DOPE

The Rumble in the Jungle was a stark demonstration of Ali's changed tactics following his return to the ring. Ali remained confident of his phenomenal speed of hand. A 1969 photographic analysis in *Sports Illustrated* magazine showed he could deliver a six-punch combination of jabs, hooks, body and head shots in just more than 2 seconds. Ali knew, though, he was slower on his feet and could no longer dance around younger opponents.

He and Angelo Dundee devised a risky tactic for the Foreman fight. Instead of trading blows toe-to-toe, Ali stayed on the ropes and let Foreman hit him! This was astounding to onlookers because Foreman was known as the all-time hardest-hitting heavyweight. Ali would then lean forward inviting a knockout head punch and rapidly lean back out of the way. Ali was well prepared to take rib and belly shots because he had spent months before leaving for Zaire in the gym practising being beaten up by sparring partners such as Larry Holmes, a future Heavyweight Champion. Also he relied on give in the ropes to limit the damage. Dundee later confessed his part in the tactic: adjusting the rope tension to help Ali use the ring edge to his advantage.

Ali called the technique rope-a-dope, but it was not new. Ironically, Archie Moore, who was in Foreman's training camp, had called the tactic of absorbing heavy punches until the time was right to counter-attack, 'the turtle'. Rope-a dope almost failed for Ali in round two when he was pinned to the ropes and appeared to wobble and grabbed Foreman's shoulder. Before round six, a Zairean official accidentally loosened the ropes – if Dundee had not noticed and told Ali, he may have leant back and fallen from the ring!

Ali is shown here on the ropes using his rope-a-dope tactic while defending against Foreman's onslaught.

BOXER FOCUS: GEORGE FOREMAN

George Foreman grew up in Texas in a poor family, and as a teenager was a mugger and brawler on the streets of Houston. He fell into boxing by chance when he was put on a job corps programme to teach vocational skills to the disadvantaged. One of the corps counsellor's was also a boxing coach and saw the punching potential in George's 6 foot 3 inch (1. 9 m), muscular frame.

George proved to be so good that he became 1968 Olympic Heavyweight Champion in his 25th amateur fight. Within three years of turning professional, he had knocked out opponents 35 times in 37 matches. By 1973, he was crowned World Champion when he floored the mighty Joe Frazier. A year later, he was defeated by Ali in Zaire, and in 1977, announced his retirement after a claimed religious experience in the dressing room following his last fight. George was ordained a minister the next year.

By the early 1980s, he was a boxing commentator for the HBO network and had set up a youth centre. However, he was short on funds so returned to professional boxing ten years after retiring.

George resumed where he left off, knocking out opponents. However, there were allegations that his promoter bribed officials to up his ranking to get a title shot, first against Evander Holyfield, which he lost on points, and then Michael Moorer in 1994. At age 45 Foreman became the oldest ever World Heavyweight Champion when he knocked out Moorer. When Foreman retired for good in 1997 he had already started promoting a range of electric cookers branded Lean Mean Grilling Machines. By 2014, an estimated 100 million Grilling Machines had been sold. Foreman continues to juggle evangelism, developing and marketing products, and running a ranch in Texas.

George Foreman at ease out of the ring.

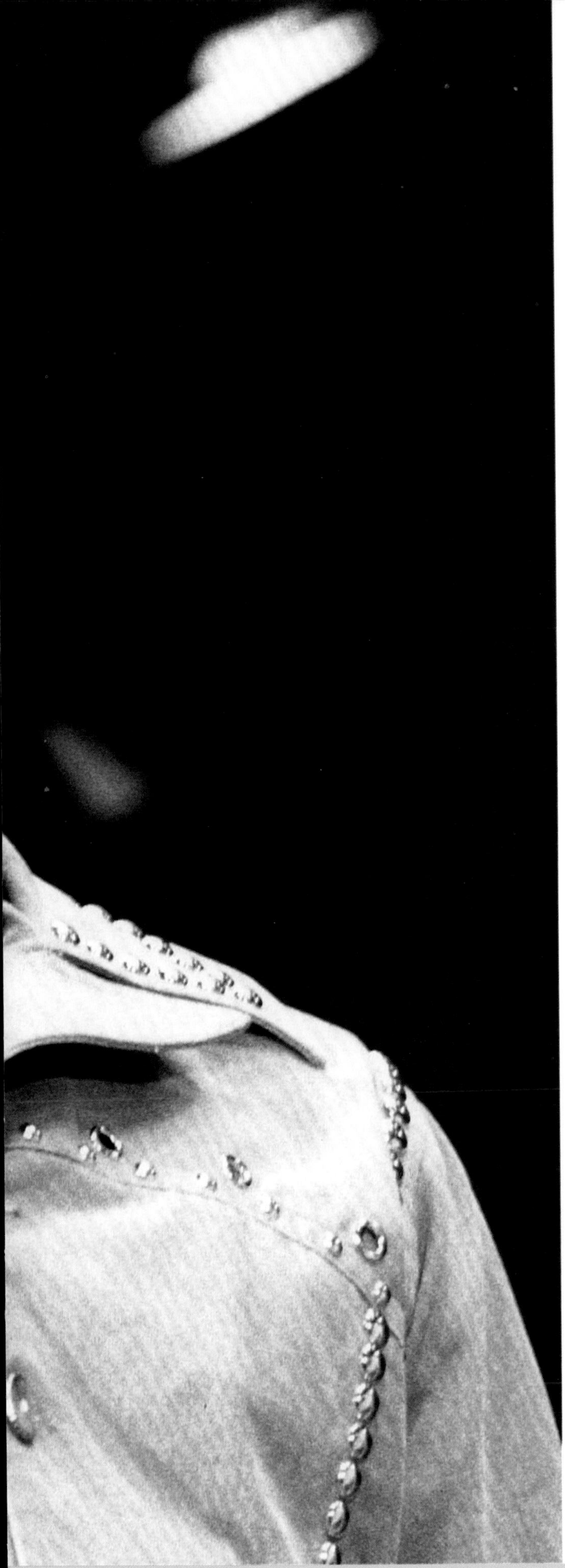

Foreman poses as he trains in 1972 in New York.

STATISTICS

BORN	Marshall (TX), January 1949
TURNED PROFESSIONAL	1969
NUMBER OF PRO BOUTS	81
WINS-LOSSES-DRAWS	76-5-0
NUMBER OF KNOCKOUTS	68
RETIRED	1997

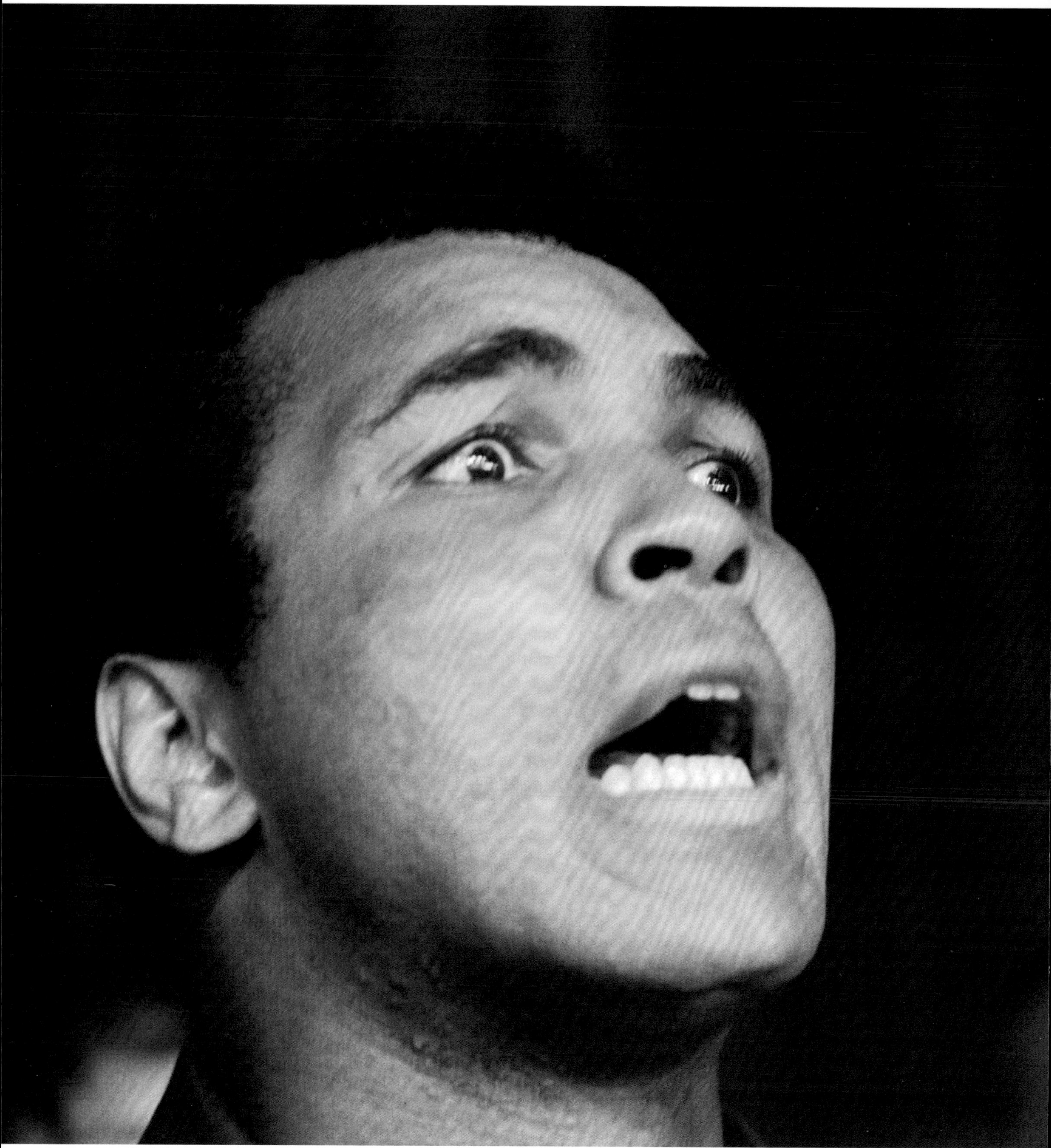

Ali in his pomp, mocking Joe Frazier's predictions of a victory, in a press conference in 1975.

RESURRECTION

Ali was now king of the boxing world and suddenly a national treasure on his return to the United States. In December 1974, he was invited to visit President Gerald Ford in the White House. Ford wanted to meet Ali as a boxing enthusiast but also out of national reconciliation now that the US troops were out of Vietnam and racial divisions were declining. He said prophetically: "Because of his principles... Muhammad Ali will be remembered for more than just excellence in athletics."

Ali became a darling of the media, featuring in many photoshoots and pictured attending numerous events. Of course, Ali fed the hero worship, reading from epic poems about his achievements such as:

"This is the legend of Muhammad Ali, the greatest fighter that ever will be."

In 1975, Elijah Muhammad died and the Nation of Islam changed course. Led by Wallace Muhammad, it stated that the Quran taught that colour does not matter and that Muslims hate any injustice and evil. Ali said: "We're in a new phase, a resurrection." This change in tack created deep divisions in the Nation and was the beginning of its end.

By now Don King was looking for the next payday after Zaire for himself and for Ali. Allegedly using mob money, King matched Ali against Chuck Wepner, 'the Bayonne Bleeder' as he often got cut. It wasn't much of a contest, but King negotiated a $1.5 million payout for Ali. Soon King had made Ali's wish come true: a return bout with Joe Frazier. Again the big match was to be held overseas, this time in Manila, Philippines, on 1 October. The country was under martial law and its autocratic leader President Ferdinand Marcos thought a sporting event would take attention away from his mistreatment of his own people.

Ali wearing a Manila Gorilla T-shirt mock punches Frazier at a press conference in Quezon City, Philippines, in front of invited television crews, reporters and boxing enthusiasts.

THRILLA IN MANILA

'It will be a killer
And a chiller
And a thrilla
When I get the gorilla
In Manila'

Ali was ruthless in his pre-match taunting of Joe Frazier. At a press conference with Frazier he mocked Frazier for saying, "gonna" not "going to" and "inta" not "into". He christened Frazier "the gorilla" and repeatedly thumped a black rubber gorilla, saying: "All night long, this is what you'll see."

Before the fight, Frazier's trainer, Eddie Futch, made plans for victory. He negotiated replacing the planned US referee with a Filipino, as the former had officiated Ali versus Frazier II and he felt had insufficiently penalised neck holding by Ali. Futch also trained his man to avoid rope-a-dope by hitting Ali's arms to weaken him. It later emerged that Frazier had a cataract in his left eye, and an arthritic left shoulder. Ali was 2-1 favourite for this battle.

The fight was an intense war of attrition in sapping tropical humidity. Ali outboxed Frazier in the first third of the bout, delivering many big punches that made Frazier wobble. In the middle third, Frazier took the upper hand. In round six he whacked Ali so hard that Ali's head turned away. In the final third, Ali took control and doled out the punishment. Frazier's left eye was closed and his right closing. In the heat, there was insufficient ice to reduce the swelling. In the 14th Frazier was a sitting duck for Ali's punches but the round finished with both men slumped in their corners.

Before the bell for the 15th, Futch threw in the towel, and Ali begged Dundee to cut his gloves off as he was done. Ali had won again – netting in the region of $6 million – but this victory had taken its toll.

In the sapping heat of the Philippines the bout ebbed and flowed between both fighters, Frazier taking the upper hand mid-fight, but Ali finishing stronger.

In this classic duel, Ali only won because he was not first to quit. Both men were completely spent at the end of the fight.

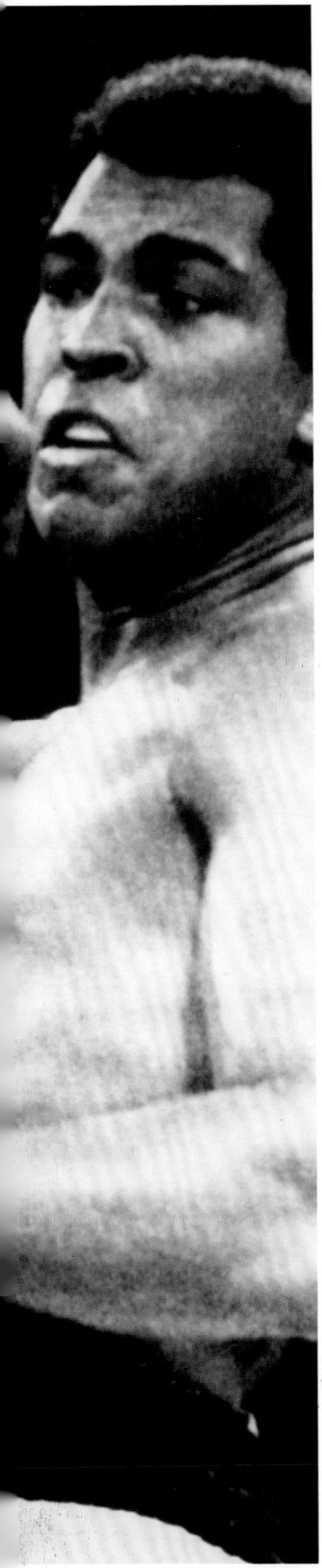

THE CLASSIC DUEL

For many people Ali v Frazier III was one of the best boxing matches in history. It was between two boxing legends who threw everything they had at each other. Ali said it was the closest to dying he had ever been. The fight had the ebb and flow of many classic fights and a gladiatorial fight-to-the-death spirit. In 1997, *The Ring* magazine awarded it, 'Fight of the Century' and in 1999, ESPN's Sports Century Series pronounced it the fifth greatest sporting event ever.

Some boxing aficionados believe the match has been overhyped, partly because Ali finally convincingly beat his nemesis, whereas in reality it was rather uninteresting. In 2012, boxing historian Mike Silvers described his sadness at seeing, "two former giants of the ring struggle and suffer."

Many people thought that Ali crossed a line in his verbal attacks on Joe Frazier out of the ring. They said that he had called Frazier ignorant, slow in speech and ugly for the sole purpose of entertaining a predominantly white audience and thus reinforced some unfortunate and persistent stereotypes about black people.

Frazier said of Ali the fighter: "In Manila, ... those punches, they'd have knocked a building down. And he took 'em... and he came back, and I got to respect that part of the man." He could never forgive how Ali tainted his image. In 1991, when Ali was first having difficulty speaking, Frazier said: "He can't talk no more because he was saying the wrong things. ... Tell me now. Him or me; which one talks worse now?" Ali himself saw the taunts as merely part of the game and retained immense respect for Frazier the warrior: "If God ever calls me to a holy war, I want Joe Frazier fighting beside me."

EVERLAST

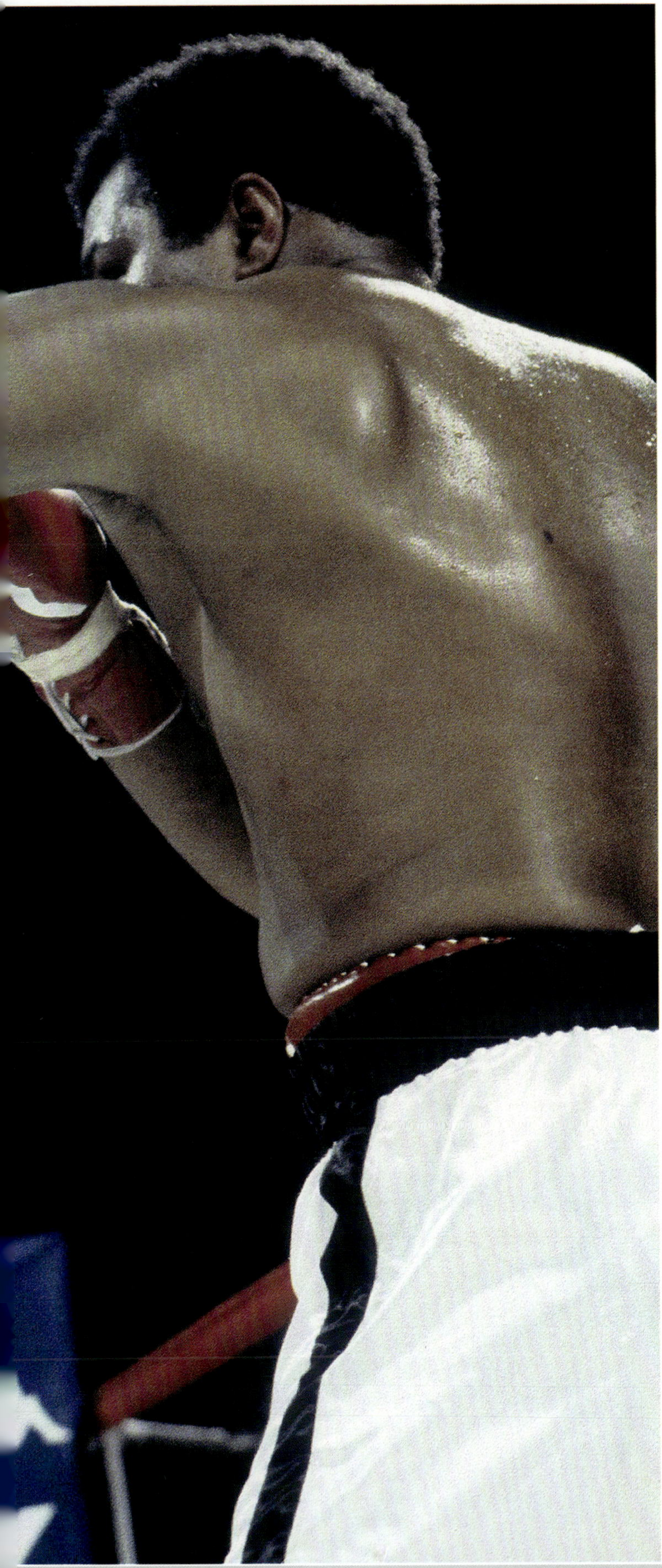

THE LAST FIGHTS

THE ALI ROAD SHOW

After beating Frazier in Manila, Muhammad Ali was probably the best-known and one of the most popular celebrities in the world. Those around him say this was not just because of his fame, but also because of his personality.

He was warm and friendly to those he met and generous to those in real need, for example handing over $100,000 dollars to save a Jewish community centre for old people, after he saw a feature about it closing due to lack of funds on the news.

Ali skipping before his World Championship bout with Jimmy Young. At this point, Ali was his heaviest weight ever and taking a lot of less-than-taxing fights against also-rans.

People loved to watch Ali fight, but they loved to watch him win more. In the years after Manila, Ali fought several opponents that did not stand a chance of beating him but were happy to fight the champion and, like him, entertain audiences while reaping great financial rewards.

On 20 February 1976, Ali fought Jean-Pierre Coopman, the heavyweight champion of Belgium. Ali justified the fight against this lesser opponent saying he needed a rest after the major workout in Manila. Coopman was so delighted to meet Ali that he kept trying to kiss him at press conferences, making it hard to build up too much drama or excitement about the event, which Ali won all too easily.

Two months later, Ali fought Jimmy Young in Maryland. Ali was slow and at 230 pounds (104 kg), he was the heaviest he had ever been. He took 15 rounds to win a fight that was universally panned as boring. Less than a month after that, Ali was on primetime television fighting England's Richard Dunn in Munich, Germany. Tickets sold badly and Ali was open to the press about his regret at having let the public down so he put on a better performance in the fight, knocking Dunn down four times before knocking him out in round five. The Ali Road Show seemed to be back in town but in reality, this was to be the champ's last ever knockout win.

The Coopman fight in Puerto Rico in 1976 was a simple workout for a boxer of Ali's skill.

POWER STRUGGLE

In the background at this time, there was a power struggle going on for the control of Ali's career. Herbert Muhammad, who was Ali's manager, was pulling away from Don King, because he believed King wanted to take over. King's efforts were to no avail however, because Herbert's friendship with Ali was so strong and long-standing, and because he distanced Ali from King, choosing promoters like Bob Arum to promote Ali's future bouts, such as his next, a controversial fight against pro-wrestler Antonio Inoki in Tokyo on 25 May 1976.

The fight was billed as a battle between the two toughest men on the planet but many viewed it as a staged circus show. When asked his reasons for taking part in a fight that many felt demeaned the boxing title, Ali was honest: "$6 million, that's why,' he replied. Nevertheless, the fighters tried to build-up some tension at press events, with Ali calling Inoki 'The Pelican' because of his big chin and Inoki presenting Ali with a crutch for after the match.

There are still disputes about whether the fight was genuine but it is known that Ali's camp renegotiated the rules of the meeting just before it took place, stating that Inoki was not allowed to do things like leg-dive or tackle. Whatever the truth, the result was 15 rounds of dull, almost farcical fighting, with Inoki bending the rules by spending much of the bout lying on the floor kicking at Ali's legs. At one point Ali tried to grab Inoki's ankle but got flipped on to the canvas with Inoki sitting on his chest and squatting over his head. The fight was scored as a draw but no one really saved face: it had been a humiliating spectacle for everyone involved. There was a cost to Ali, too: blood clots and muscle damage in his legs from all those kicks.

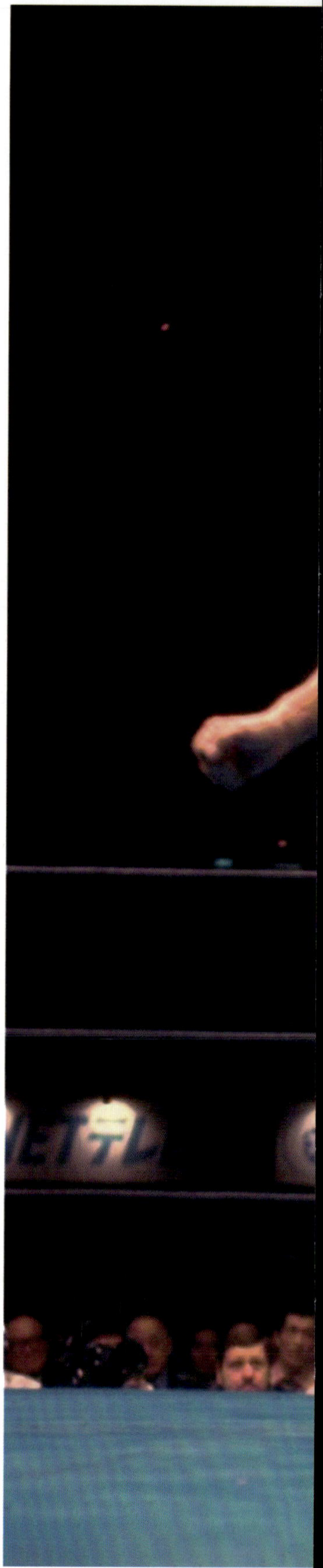

Inoki shown mid-air for a double foot drop kick – the big-money exhibition fight had a high cost for Ali: his famously powerful legs took such a beating, that Ali's movement was probably permanently slowed.

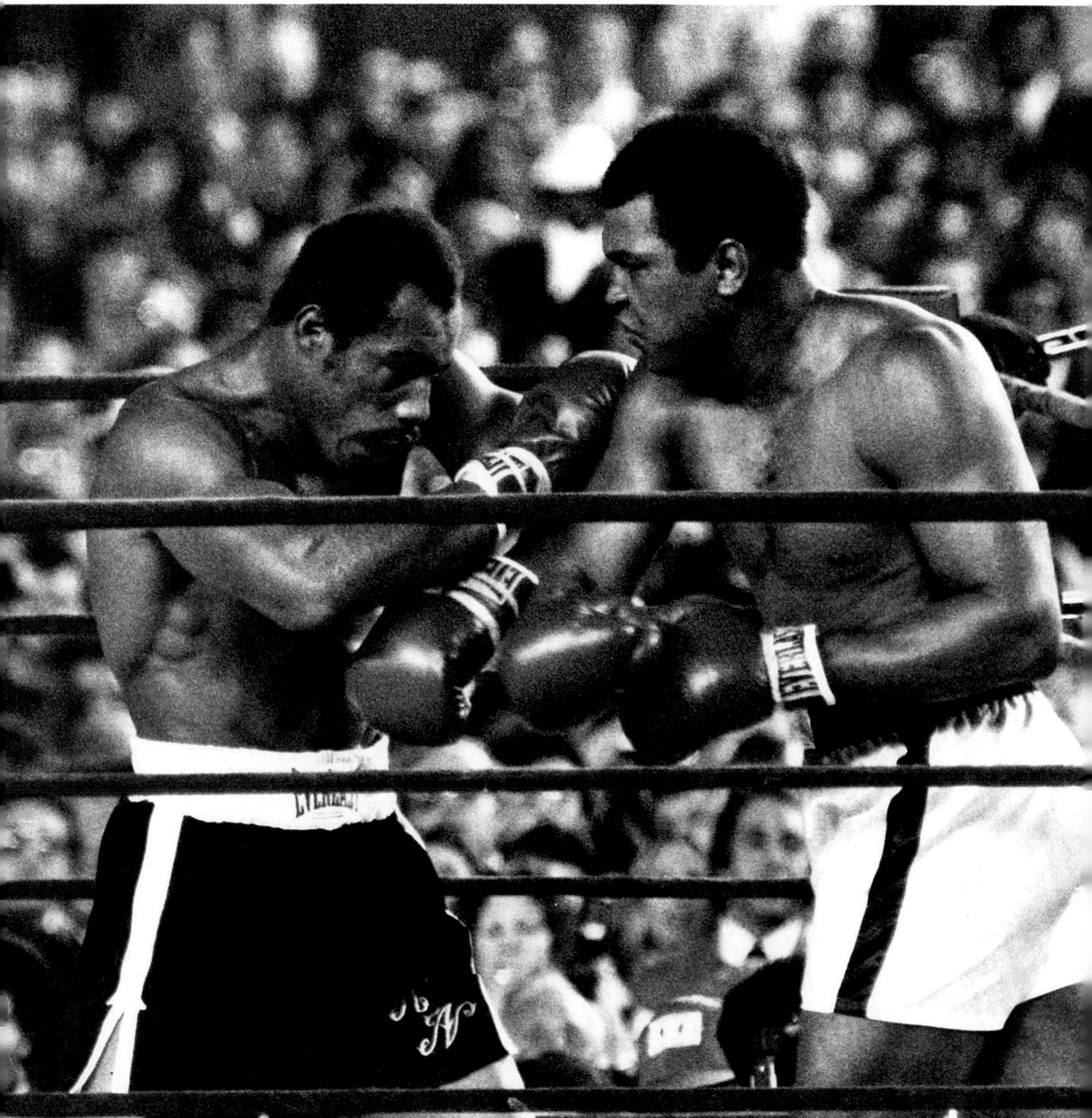

The powerhouse Ken Norton defends himself against an Ali blow during their 1976 encounter. Ali took revenge for the jaw-busting points defeat of 1973 but was a less-than-convincing victor.

ALI V NORTON

Bob Arum and Ferdie Pacheco were worried by infections to Ali's leg injuries, yet Ali spent a minimal period in hospital before starting to train for a bout against Ken Norton at Yankee Stadium, on 28 September 1976. Norton dominated the early rounds, but after round eight the tables turned as Ali, with superhuman effort, started to claw his way back. Ali, spurred on by Dundee, won the next three rounds, lost round 12, and won the next two, making the fight even by round 15. He won on a close and disputed points decision. It was clear to all that the leg problems had taken their toll on Ali's mobility.

Ali did not step into the ring again until spring 1977, for what proved to be a tedious win against Spanish newcomer Alfredo Evangelista. Even Ali was more interested in what was going on outside the ring, where his marriage to Belinda was breaking up, he had a nine-month-old child with his soon-to-be new wife Veronica, and an autobiography and a movie of his life, *The Greatest,* about to be released. It seemed that Ali's focus was on his personal ventures, not his boxing.

Just as people were speculating that Ali might retire, he booked a fight against Earnie Shavers on 29 September 1977, at Madison Square Garden. Shavers was tough and Ali was out of shape, but Ali fought 15 hard rounds to scrape another win. However, he had been hammered in the head by Shaver's brain-jarring punches so many times he suffered severe head trauma and other injuries. Several prominent people called for Ali to retire before permanent damage was done, including Pacheco, for whom the Shavers fight was the final straw. When Ali refused to stop fighting after this, his doctor of 15 years quit.

Ali makes a breakthrough against Norton.

BOXER FOCUS: KEN NORTON

Ken Norton was born and brought up in Jacksonville, Illinois, the son of a fire service engineer and a hospital therapist. After school, Norton won a football scholarship to Northeast Missouri State College. He didn't start boxing until after he joined the Marine Corps in 1963. He was a formidable athlete who took to the sport quickly.

Norton turned professional after taking the All-Marine Heavyweight Champion title three times during his four-year stint in the forces. He fought many great fighters in his time, including George Foreman, for the title in 1974. He also put his 6 foot 3 inch (1.92 m), 220 pound (99.7 kg) physique to good financial use by starring in Hollywood films such as *Mandingo* (1975), with Susan George, and *Drum* (1976), with Pam Grier, as well as television shows including *The A-Team* and *Knight Rider*.

Norton was bitterly disappointed when he lost to Ali in 1976, but he went on to take three wins in 1977 against the likes of Duane Bobick and Jimmy Young, and became the mandatory challenger for WBC Heavyweight Champion Leon Spinks, who claimed the title in 1978. The World Boxing Council stripped Spinks of the title and awarded it to Norton instead after the former agreed to a rematch with the ageing Ali instead of Norton. Norton lost the title to Larry Holmes in June the same year, after an intense 15-round fight ending in a split decision. Norton was never the same fighter again.

In 1986, Norton almost died in a car accident in which he suffered multiple injuries, including a fractured skull and a brain injury that left his speech slurred. He died after a long period of declining health, after a succession of strokes and a heart attack, since which he'd lived in a care home.

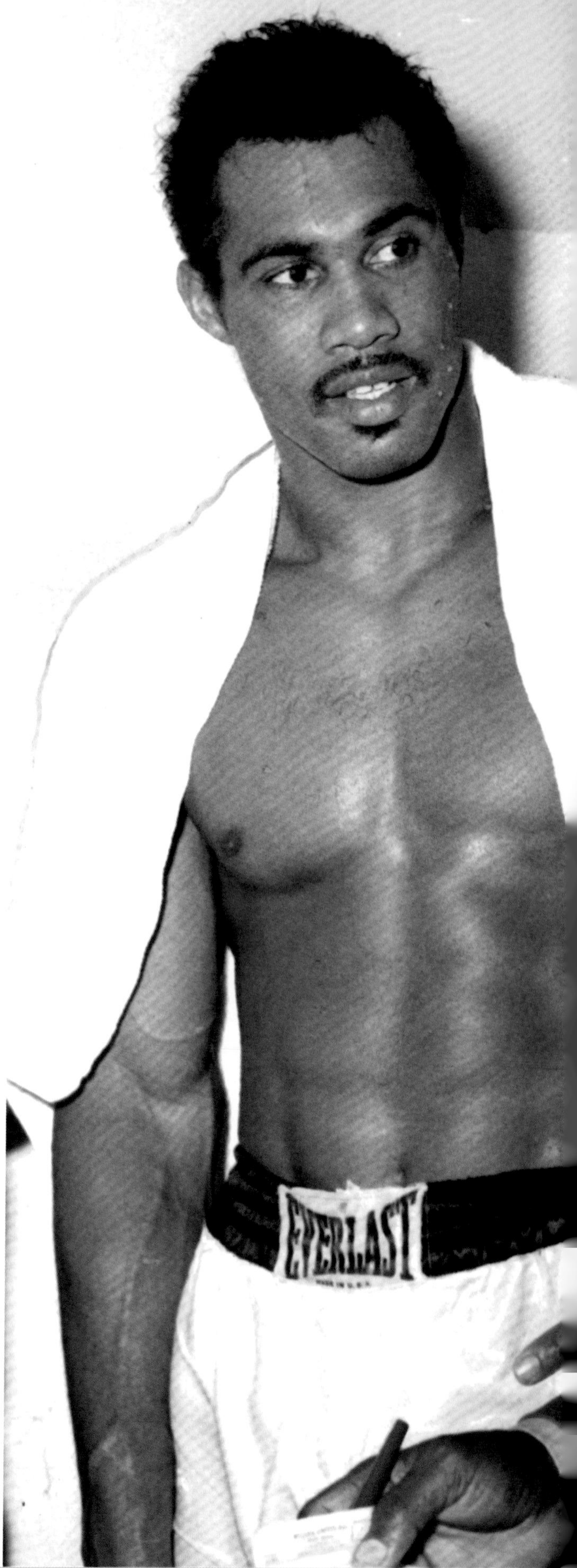

A young Ken Norton (centre) with Joe Frazier (right) in 1950.

Norton chalks up a win against Ron Stander in early 1976, before his Ali rematch.

STATISTICS

BORN	Jacksonville (IL), 9 August 1943
DIED	18 September 2013
TURNED PROFESSIONAL	1967
NUMBER OF PRO BOUTS	50
WINS-LOSSES-DRAWS	42-7-1
NUMBER OF KNOCKOUTS	33
RETIRED	1981

ALI V SPINKS

Ali's next match was in February 1978 in Las Vegas against Leon Spinks, an Olympic gold medal winner who only had seven professional bouts to his name. Ali seized the chance to take down another gold medal winner and declare himself the greatest again, but he did not bother training much, assuming it would be an easy win. It wasn't. Spinks was young and strong and went on punching Ali for the entire 15 rounds, never tiring as Ali expected. Ali tried to make a comeback in the final round but it was too late. The judges awarded the win and Ali's World Heavyweight title to Spinks. The loss hurt Ali badly and as soon as the fight was over, Ali was calling for another, to win back his title.

The rematch was arranged for 15 September that year in New Orleans. Ali began training harder than he had ever trained in his life, including sparring more than 200 rounds in the ring. On the day, Ali soon settled into his rhythm, moving and punching solidly and using improvised moves that could only come from a fighter of his experience. Over the course of the match, he jabbed and hooked with ever increasing confidence and accuracy. He even displayed the odd speedy and devastating mix of hooks and uppercuts, and landed overhand rights, which left his opponent frustrated and helpless. Ali won by unanimous decision and at 36 years old, became the first three-time Heavyweight Champion in history.

After the match, Ali said: "I've always planned to be the first black man to retire undefeated, and to do it now after being champion three times would be something no one could ever equal. I have made suckers out of all of you." He announced his retirement the following June.

Ali backs away from a punch thrown by Leon Spinks during their 15 September 1978 bout in the Superdome, New Orleans. Ali trained incredibly hard to make sure he did not make the same mistakes as before against Spinks.

BOXER FOCUS: LEON SPINKS

Leon Spinks was born in a rough area of St. Louis, Missouri, and brought up by his mother on welfare assistance. He left school after the tenth grade and went into the US Marine Corps where he joined the All-Marine boxing team. He won light heavyweight bronze at the World Games in Cuba in 1974, silver at the Pan-American Games in 1975, and gold at the 1976 Summer Olympics in Montreal. His brother Michael won gold in the middleweight, making them the first brothers in history to be champions in the same sport at the same Olympics.

In 1977, Spinks turned professional and moved up to the heavyweight division. He took the World Heavyweight title from Muhammad Ali in 1978, in one of the greatest upsets in boxing history, but was stripped of the title after agreeing to fight Ali rather than the number-one contender: Norton. In 1981, Spinks challenged Larry Holmes for the title but lost in three rounds. His last championship chance was in 1986 when he fought Dwight Qawi at cruiserweight level but he lost in six rounds. Financial problems forced Spinks to continue fighting autograph shows and boxer-versus-wrestler matches long past his prime until he retired in 1995.

Although he and Michael were the first brothers in boxing history to win World Heavyweight titles (Michael defeated Larry Holmes in the IBF Heavyweight Championship in 1985), their later lives took divergent paths. Michael Spinks left boxing with his health and his money. Leon Spinks allegedly squandered his winnings on alcohol and gambling, and for a while was homeless and living in a shelter. Since then he has worked in restaurants, at a YMCA and has done other odd jobs. He has also helped to start a gym in Detroit, and in Nebraska, he volunteers at an after-school programme for youth.

Spinks in training before his first Ali fight, which catapulted him to boxing stardom.

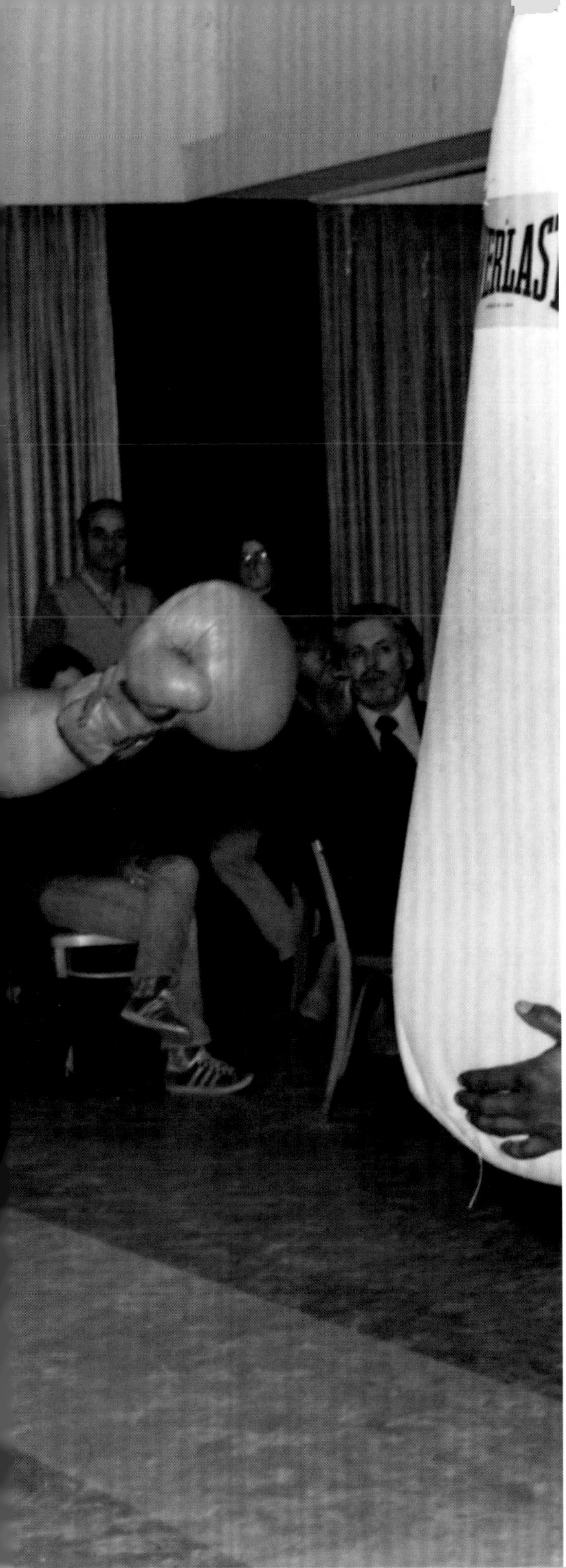

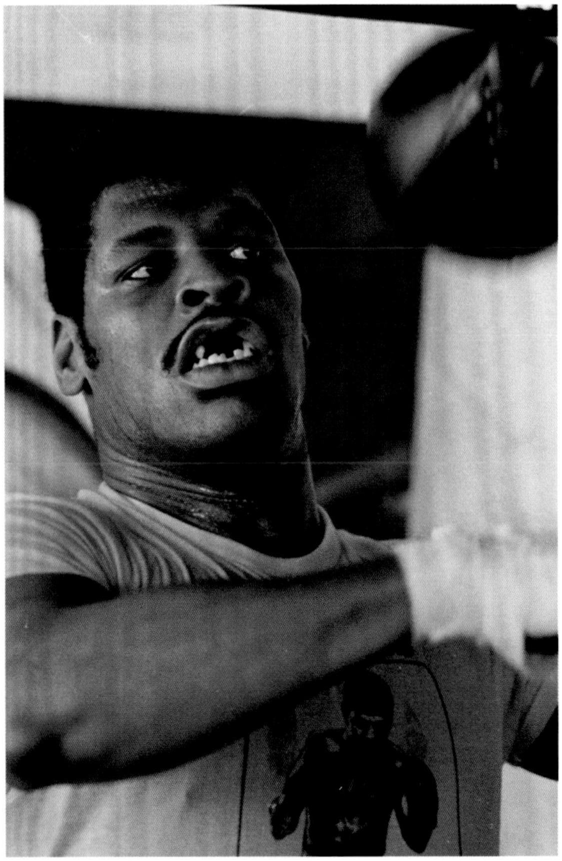

Spinks had his front teeth loosened by boxing and then removed in 1971 while in the marines. He often wore false front teeth, but they were sometimes stolen as trophies!

STATISTICS

BORN	St. Louis (MO), 11 July 1953
TURNED PROFESSIONAL	1977
NUMBER OF PRO BOUTS	46
WINS-LOSSES-DRAWS	26-17-3
NUMBER OF KNOCKOUTS	14
RETIRED	1995

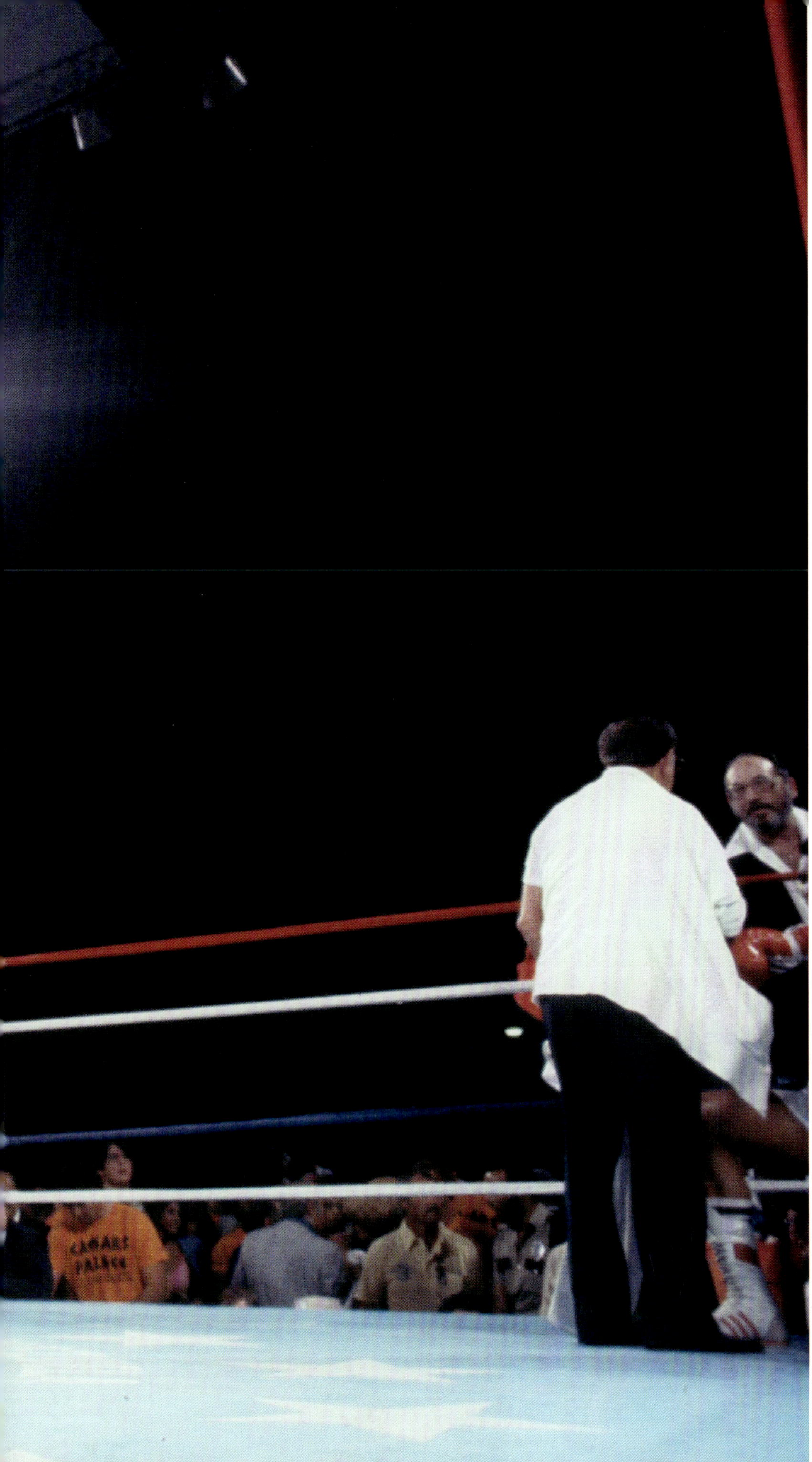

Larry Holmes stands victorious over Ali, who sits hurt and beaten in his corner.

THE LAST FIGHT

After the Spinks victory, Ali concentrated on other projects for a while. He played an ex-slave in a four-hour television mini-series called *Freedom Road*, with Kris Kristofferson, he moved into a huge, luxurious mansion in Las Vegas, and he travelled the world, for example to India to raise money for Indian charities. In 1979, after Russia invaded Afghanistan, President Carter asked him to visit countries in Africa to represent the United States' reasons for boycotting the Moscow Olympics.

Ali was soon planning to get back in the ring. He did it partly for the money, because although he'd earned millions over his career, he had spent a lot, given away a lot of it, and had been conned out of some, but also because he loved the roar of the crowd, loved to fight and to show people he could still win.

On 2 October 1980, and in spite of public statements issued by his mother and former doctor, Pacheco, saying he should not return to boxing, Ali stepped out of retirement and into the ring at Caesars Palace, Las Vegas, to face Larry Holmes, a former sparring partner and current heavyweight champion.

It was a disaster. Ali never had a dominant moment in the fight, but he would not stop or drop. He just absorbed the severe beatings that Holmes dished out. In round nine, an uppercut from Holmes threw Ali against the ropes and as Ali turned away and covered his face with his gloves, Holmes delivered a right hand to his kidney that made Ali scream with pain. After round ten, Ali's trainer, Angelo Dundee, finally stopped the sad spectacle. This time there was no denying that Ali was in terminal decline.

Ali eyeballed Trevor Berbick in vain at the weigh-in in Nassau, the Bahamas, but many knew his boxing days were near the end and he did not have the moves to back up his pre-match talk. Berbick would prove to be his last ever boxing opponent.

Ali was hurt in more ways than one after the Holmes disaster. He refused to accept the decision and wanted to prove his worth in the ring. At the age of 39 he was fixated with the idea of becoming champ for a fourth time: "Why do people go to the moon? Why did Martin Luther King say he had a dream? People need challenges."

In September 1981, a ten-round fight against the Jamaican-Canadian, Trevor Berbick, was announced. Berbick had recently lost closely to Holmes, too. But US boxing commissions were officially concerned about the state of Ali's health and would not sanction the fight on US soil. US networks were not interested in televising the bout, planned for Nassau, the Bahamas, and promoted by a Bahamian company, Sports Internationale. They tagged it 'The Drama in Bahama'. Pre-fight things were shoddy – ringside tickets were on sale in a supermarket and there were concerns Sports Internationale would go bust. In early December, to soothe anxieties about the fight, Ali publicly released a medical report from UCLA Medical Center stating: "There is no evidence from a health standpoint that he should be limited whatsoever in his activities."

On the evening of 11 December Ali and Berbick stepped into the ring. Shambolic organisation meant the referees had to ask around for a stopwatch and bell. Ali looked fresh at the start, dancing round and flicking jabs, but it was immediately apparent that he could not move out of the way of Berbick's solid head shots. By round three he was tiring. Ali traded blows but they had little effect on the 27-year-old. Ali's reactions and speed had gone and he could not dodge Berbick's blows. He put off the inevitable until the final bell: a Berbick victory. This sad fight was the last in Ali's auspicious career in the ring.

A SECOND LIFE

RETIREMENT

"Father Time caught up with me. I'm finished. I've got to face the facts. For the first time I could feel that I'm 40 years old."

In the press conference in Nassau the morning after Berbick fight, Berbick described beating Ali as his, "great honour and also a sad one". However, journalists were far more interested in the main story: the end of Ali's boxing career. At the conference Ali teased Berbick for beating up an old man and proclaimed Berbick, "as good as any man I ever fought". But out of Berbick's earshot he said: "If I was 27, Trevor would have been my sparring partner."

Ali said he would have retired even if he had won because he felt conclusively that during the rounds he could not, "make certain attacks". At the end of the conference, to everyone's surprise, he suddenly pronounced: "I shall return!" But then added: "To Los Angeles", where he lived.

For Ali the early 1980s were difficult times. He had the trappings of success such as an enormous mansion, he had a glorious boxing record, international renown, and had met a pantheon of famous people. But he was bereft to be out of the boxing cycle of talking up his chances against opponents, training, competing and so on. Angelo Dundee said: "He met every big name in the world but what really energised him was being around fight guys." He knew he had left the ring with a whimper rather than a roar and that the boxing world believed he had brought the sport into some disrepute by fighting on when he was not really able. Ali retained close advisors who organised public appearances, but he was no longer surrounded by a large entourage. For the first time in years, Ali felt all alone.

Muhammad Ali with actor Tony Curtis in 1982.

When Ali visited China in 1985, he was already suffering from the effects of Parkinson's disease.

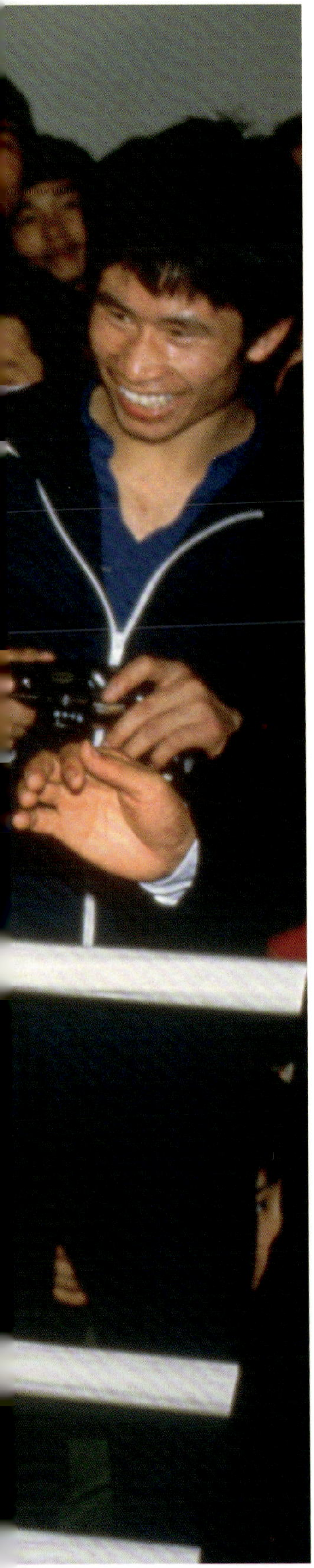

ILLNESS

Ali knew he was struggling with neurological symptoms before his last fights. At the time of the 1980 UCLA report, he blamed the symptoms on the thyroid pills that he took to help lose weight before the Holmes fight. He kept quiet the findings of a report from the Denver Mayo Clinic, which found he could not accurately touch his finger to his nose tip, he had trouble coordinating speech and could not hop well on one foot. Publicly he kept up pretences that all was OK: "You listen to me talk. Do I sound like I've got brain damage to you?"

After retirement Ali's health was under great scrutiny. It was apparent that his speech was more slurred than in the past, he moved more slowly and had tremors. He had many more tests at leading neurological institutions in the United States over the following years, and finally a PET scan in 1984 revealed that Ali had damage to his brain stem. This, along with response to medication and other tests, confirmed that he had Parkinson's Disease. Parkinson's symptoms, from tremor, slowness and rigidity to fatigue, pain and sleeplessness, result from the brain not producing a neurotransmitter called dopamine.

Parkinson's resulting from head trauma has been the prevailing theory since Ali's diagnosis, especially given that other boxers, including Sugar Ray Leonard, have also suffered neurological damage post-career. Many people blame the punishing later fights including those with Frazier and Holmes. Henry Cooper blamed it on Ali's fighting style: "We were always taught as kids that you never turned your head on a punch... But [Ali] used to turn, and he took [too] many punches to the back of the head." However, Parkinson's has many causes, from family history to viruses and exposure to toxins. Some doctors think Ali may have got the disease even without stepping into the ring.

PUBLIC APPEARANCES

After the world finally knew for sure that Ali was suffering from Parkinson's, the ex-champion reassured people that he was far from finished and that he would get on with life. He said that on Parkinson's medication to lessen the symptoms, he felt fine and that he was in no pain, even though he admitted that he was, "older and fatter, but we all change." Ali remained firmly in the public eye.

In 1985, Ali got back in the ring but this time, a wrestling ring. The event was called WrestleMania, which was held at Madison Square Garden – the scene of some of Ali's most famous fights. The main event in this pay-per-view match was a tag-team bout between the professional wrestler Hulk Hogan and the television actor Mr T against 'Rowdy' Roddy Piper and 'Mr. Wonderful' Paul Orndorff. The 19,000 crowd saw Ali dressed as referee, along with Liberace as timekeeper, introduce the wrestlers. Ali did not actually stay in the ring to referee, fearful of being bowled over by the wrestlers but he remained ringside to mock-punch people thrown from the ring. He held Hogan's hand aloft in victory at the end.

Ali retained a strong interest in heavyweight boxing and in particular, the emergence of Mike Tyson. In 1985, Mike Tyson had just turned professional at age 18 and was setting the heavyweight world on fire. In about 1977, Ali had inspired Tyson to focus on boxing when he visited the detention centre in the Bronx where Tyson was staying. Tyson was also promoted by Don King. In 1986, he became the youngest world champion in history when he knocked out Trevor Berbick, who was by then trained by Ali's close friend Dundee.

Ali is shown getting ready to participate as a guest referee in the inaugural Wrestlemania at Madison Square Garden, New York, in 1985.

Ali poses with released hostage Royce Smart, on 4 December 1990 after the latter's arrival at Kennedy International Airport.

MEETING SADDAM

In August 1990, Iraqi military forces invaded Kuwait and annexed it as part of Iraq. Saddam Hussein, the Iraqi leader, said it was retaliation against Kuwait drilling into their oil reserves. NATO condemned the invasion and the United States threatened Saddam with war if he did not withdraw Iraqi forces. Saddam took Western hostages to act as a 'human shield' to prevent military strikes on Iraq. The United States used sanctions and also took part in diplomatic moves to try to release US hostages. One venture, organised by a former US Attorney General, was sending 'celebrity diplomats' to Baghdad to meet with Saddam to try to make him release captives. Ali was asked to be one of those diplomats.

Ali arrived in Baghdad in November 1990. He was well-known in the Middle East owing to his very public Muslim faith and his past history of standing up to his own government. He was considered a reasonable person to with whom to negotiate. Ali met people on Baghdad's streets and in schools, and visited important holy shrines. He waited a week before Saddam would meet him, in which time he ran out of his Parkinson's medication, making it difficult to talk.

Back in the United States some questioned his presence in Baghdad: was he there for self-promotion? Did he break sanctions by negotiating with Saddam? According to Ali, Saddam was a 'man of conviction' and accepted the logic that hostage release would be, "good for maintaining peace in the area". Ali managed to negotiate the release of 15 hostages, whom he accompanied back to the United States in December 1990. He said of Iraq that it was, "the Garden of Eden" and should not be bombed. He was unaware that Saddam was releasing hostages anyway because he had now built up sufficient Iraqi forces to fight a war. He was unaware, too that President George Bush was intent on fighting that war regardless of hostage release. In February 1991, US forces invaded Iraq in Operation Desert Storm.

NATION'S HONOURS

"I've always wanted to be more than just a boxer. More than just the three-time Heavyweight Champion. I wanted to use my fame, and this face that everyone knows so well, to help uplift and inspire people around the world."

In the wilderness of the late 1970s and through the later boxing years, few people in the US government or US organisations wanted to have much to do with Muhammad Ali. How things had changed then when Ali, sporting a white tracksuit, slowly jogged carrying a torch. He used it to send a flaming arrow that lit the Olympic flame in Atlanta, Georgia, in the opening ceremony of the summer games in 1996. This was symbolic of his return from the cold, especially as he was given a gold medal. This was to replace the one he supposedly threw away after his Rome victory in 1960. Ali's part in an Olympic ceremony was to be repeated in 2012 at the London Games, but this time he helped to carry the Olympic flag from a wheelchair, aided by his wife Lonnie.

Ali had been officially recognised earlier than 1996 by his nation, for non-sporting reasons. In 1987, he was selected by the California Bicentennial Foundation for the U.S. Constitution as someone who personified the vitality of the Bill of Rights in striving for the equality of each person before God, and the responsibility of government to secure the rights of all. In 2005, Ali was awarded the Presidential Medal of Freedom in 2005, which is the highest civil award in the United States, in recognition of, "his lifetime of achievement and for his principled service to mankind." In 2012, Ali won the Liberty Medal for embracing the ideals of the US constitution. President Bill Clinton said: "Ali embodies the spirit of the Liberty Medal by embracing the ideals of the Constitution – freedom, self-governance, equality and empowerment – and helping to spread them across the globe."

Ali holds the torch before lighting the Olympic flame during the Opening Ceremony of the 1996 Centennial Olympic Games in Atlanta, Georgia.

INTERNATIONAL WORK

In 1998, at a brief ceremony in New York, UN Secretary General Kofi Annan pinned a dove of peace badge to Ali's lapel and named him a Messenger of Peace. This high honour was recognition of his global pursuit of peace outside the boxing ring.

Ali had spoken against inequalities in South Africa at the UN nearly 20 years earlier at a Special Committee against apartheid. In 1993, he went to South Africa on a benevolent mission and met Nelson Mandela who had been recently released from jail. In 2013, he paid tribute to Mandela, who he said had reached for the impossible in uniting South Africa and "taught us forgiveness on a grand scale".

Ali has widely preached and acted to help those in need. As UN messenger of Peace, he took part in missions to raise awareness of the needs of people in the internationally vilified countries of Afghanistan and North Korea. In Afghanistan, Ali visited a UNICEF-backed girls' school, a rare institution as pupils and teachers were in danger from Taliban forces that banned the education of women. He also gave support to a women's bakery that employed widows of war, and a Kabul boxing club where photographs of his fighting days decorated the walls.

Ali, in his role as UN Messenger of Peace, arrives at Kabul Airport, Afghanistan, for a three-day goodwill mission in 2002.

Ali has helped to distribute food and medical supplies to Cuba during the years of US embargo, to street children in Morocco, and to a refugee orphanage in Ivory Coast. More generally he has worked with the World Food Programme and helped to facilitate more than 200 million meals for the world's hungry. In the United States he has visited and fundraised numerous ventures, from soup kitchens and hospitals to summer camps for disadvantaged children and adoption agencies. Ali may have raised more for US charities than any other single person. Little wonder that for the breadth of his humanitarian work, Ali was granted an Amnesty lifetime achievement award.

Actress Julia Roberts shares a joke with Ali at the Amnesty International Media Spotlight Awards. There, Ali received a lifetime achievement award.

Ali and fellow Parkinson's sufferer Michael J. Fox are seen here in Washington, where they asked the Senate for more funds for Parkinson's research.

MUHAMMAD ALI PARKINSON CENTER

Jimmy Walker is a philanthropist who made his money through financial planning and investments in sports teams such as the Phoenix Giants baseball team in the 1980s. As a trustee on the Barrow Neurological Foundation, he came up with the idea of using his contacts in sports and other media to help raise funds for and awareness about a new unit specialising in treatment of Parkinson's disease. The unit was being set up by Dr. Abraham Lieberman. Lieberman has been Ali's physician since his diagnosis with Parkinson's Disease in the mid-1980s, seeing him every other week since then, and is an authority on the disease. Lieberman said: "Jimmy had the idea that if Muhammad had his name in the event, it would be a bigger deal... He's the greatest sports figure of the 20th century and I think the fact that he has Parkinson's disease makes people much more aware."

Lieberman realised that there was a pressing need for a more holistic approach to treating the disease. Rather than having patients diagnosed in one place, treated in another and having disconnected access to strategies for living with Parkinson's, the Center brought together clinical and research expertise on Parkinson's with its treatment, from using surgery such as stimulation of brain movement centres to therapies, including drugs, and teaching tactics for living with the progressive disease.

Ali was a rich man when he was diagnosed with Parkinson's and could afford to see the best medical experts, wherever they were located. He was also prey to suspicious medical advice at times, such as blood filtering to remove pesticides that some experts thought were causing his Parkinson's syndromes. So he endorsed having everything in one place, run by respected experts, and the Center's emphasis on promoting community integration and outreach, through recreational therapy programs and excellence in education about Parkinson's, for people at the thin end of the wedge – patients and caregivers.

CELEBRITY FIGHT NIGHT

In 1994, a celebrity charity fundraising event was organised in Phoenix, again by Jimmy Walker, the philanthropist. Invited wealthy guests and charity workers in tuxedoes and glamorous dresses witnessed a humorous fight in a boxing ring between two stars of local Phoenix Suns basketball team, Charles Barkley and Dan Majerle, wearing outsize boxing gloves. Auctions of objects and experiences, ticket and drinks takings raised $100,000. It was a smash hit and the next year, a long set by singer Kenny Rogers helped the event morph into an evening of entertainment. In 1996, Muhammad Ali was invited as the featured guest.

Ali's involvement upped the stakes for Celebrity Fight Night. His global name in boxing and in other fields proved a real draw for celebrities. Ali used the spotlight in 1996 to tell the world about the Muhammad Ali Parkinson Center. Since then the Center has become the focal charity for the event and has received some $45 million in donations from Celebrity Fight Night. Each year, The Muhammad Ali Celebrity Fight Night Awards, are presented to leaders in the sports, entertainment and business communities who best represent the qualities associated with Ali and his fight to find a cure for Parkinson's disease. Recipients have included Halle Berry, Arnold Schwarzenegger, fellow Parkinson's sufferer Michael J. Fox and boxer Evander Holyfield. Entertainment is kept at a high standard by multi-Grammy winner David Foster, featuring such global stars as Celine Dion, Lionel Richie, Gloria Estefan and Jennifer Lopez.

By 2013, Celebrity Fight Night had become one of the highest grossing charity events in the United States. No wonder, with tickets selling at up to $5,000 and auctions for unique experiences, such as a night with Jennifer Lopez on the red carpet in Hollywood, dinner with Billy Crystal and Robert De Niro in New York, or lunch and golf with golfer Phil Mickelson.

Ali and wife Lonnie attend Muhammad Ali's Celebrity Fight Night in Phoenix, Arizona in 2013.

THE BIOPIC

In 1994, the idea of a biopic about Ali was kicking around Hollywood. The original screenplay by Gregory Allen Howard focused on the troubled relationship between Ali and his father Cassius Sr. Directors including Oliver Stone and Steven Spielberg had contemplated making it. The charismatic young film star Will Smith was identified to play Ali but he refused as the screenplay was controversial and Ali was so universally scrutinised, saying "I didn't want to be the dude that messed up the Muhammad Ali story."

That changed in the late 1990s when a new script emerged by *Forrest Gump* screenwriter, Eric Roth, and director Michael Mann came on board. Smith confessed: "If there's a role I was born to play, this is it," and Ali said at their first meeting: "Man, you're almost pretty enough to play me." Smith immersed himself in the role by watching endless interviews with Ali to perfect the voice and getting fighting fit. He entered a professional training camp with Sugar Ray Leonard's trainer, Darrell Foster, running 3 miles (4.8 km) and boxing for 2 hours each morning, watching fight films and then lifting weights to bulk up. At the end of the camp, Foster said Smith "could fight for real. His hand speed's real good."

Mann filmed scenes as authentically as possible. For example, he recreated the Rumble in the Jungle in a football stadium in Mozambique, with a crowd of 20,000 volunteers and 2,000 paid extras plus, some cardboard cutouts! Sony Pictures was so worried about the budget that they temporarily pulled out until Mann and Smith took partial financial risk in the project. Ali opened in 2001. It had cost $100 million to make but recouped a tenth of this on opening weekend. Ali said at the Louisville premiere: "It's a great movie. Will Smith did a great job."

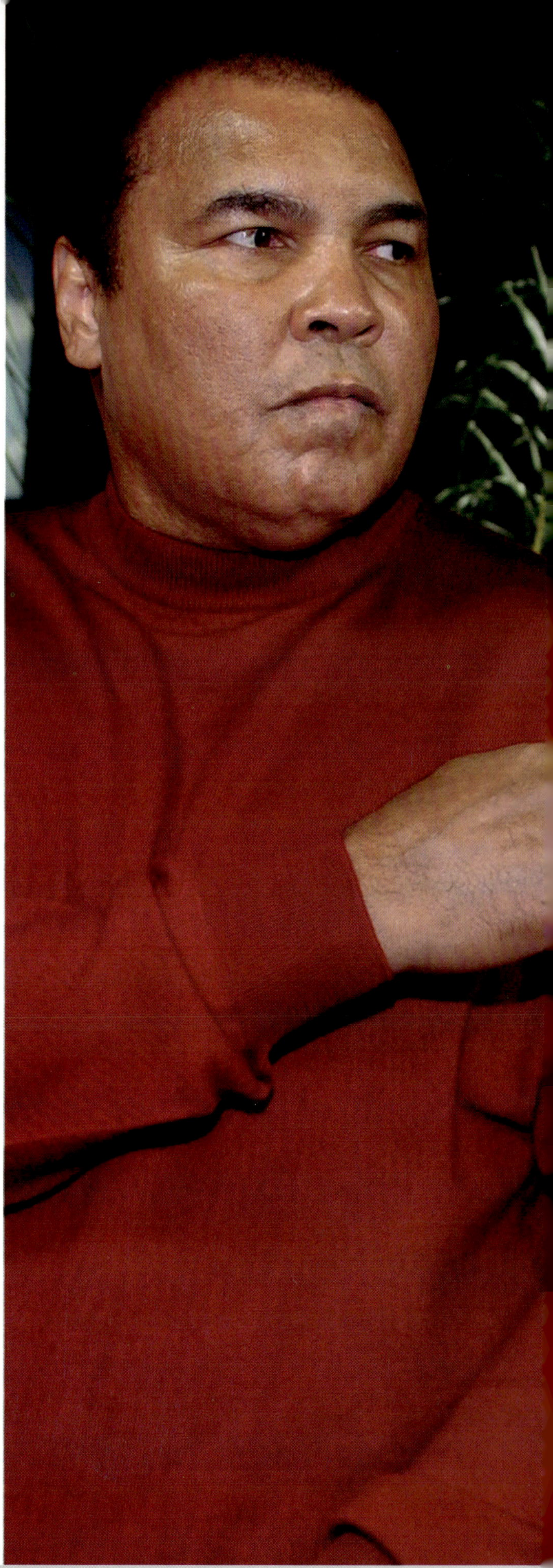

Actor Will Smith portraying Ali in a fight scene from *Ali*.

Ali jokes with US actor Will Smith, who plays him in the film *Ali* at the film's premiere in Hollywood in 2001, watched by Smith's son.

Ali holds a flame with former Heavyweight Champion Evander Holyfield during the Grand Opening Gala for the Muhammad Ali Center in Louisville in 2005.

MUHAMMAD ALI CENTER

"A visitor of the Muhammad Ali Center experiences the hows of Ali's life: how he found the courage, the dedication, and the discipline to become who he is today; how he found the conviction to stand up for what he believed; and how he turned his passion for excellence in the ring to a passion for peace on the world stage."

The other big charitable cause in Ali's life is his eponymous center in his home city of Louisville, Kentucky. Ali had always retained strong links with the place where he grew up, which had celebrated him in different ways, from naming a street after him in 1978 to naming him the greatest athlete of all time in 2000. Ali co-founded the Center in 2005 with his wife Lonnie. At its heart is an interactive museum about Ali but its mission is to promote respect, hope and understanding, and inspire greatness, in the spirit of Ali's life.

The Center is linked to the Muhammad Ali Institute for Peace and Justice at the University of Louisville. This advances the study and practice of social justice, peace building and violence prevention. It does this through initiatives such as SeeRedNow, an educational media campaign designed to encourage better understanding of root causes of violence, and The Ali Scholars Program for undergraduates to travel internationally to explore, witness and collaborate in peace and social justice work.

Funding for the Center came from the city from an anonymous donor and Ford Motor Company. City leaders invested in the project as part of urban re-development of downtown Louisville. However, the project is not without controversy. Critics have questioned the building of the Center downtown, rather than in the predominantly black, run-down West End part of the city, where Ali grew up and where re-development would have arguably had a greater impact, and the Center's goals would have had greater relevance.

The Muhammad Ali Center, in Louisville, Kentucky.

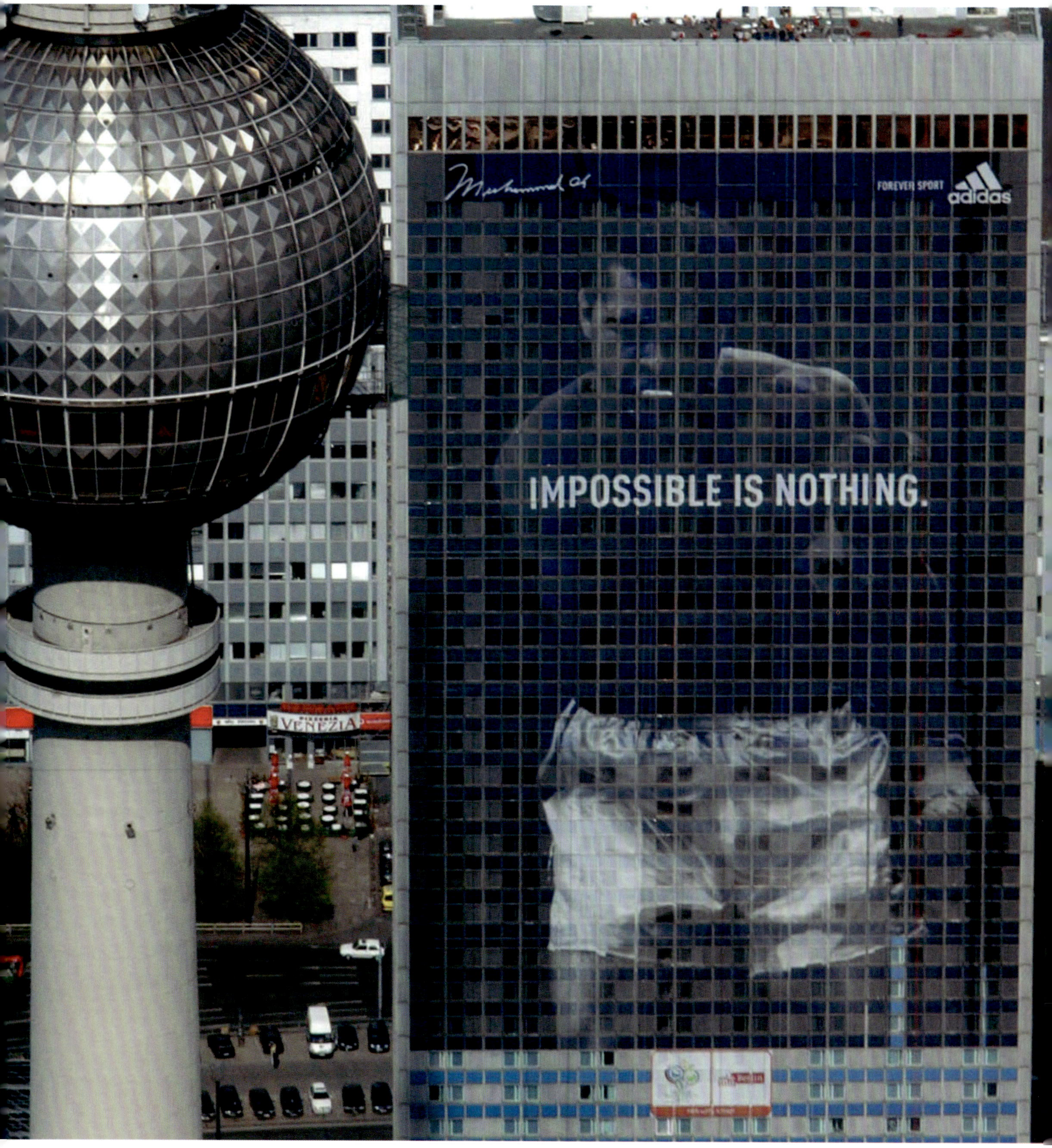

In 2004, sports company Adidas created this 1,544 square mile (4,000 m2) advert using a portrait of Ali, which covered the façade of the Berlin Park Inn.

BRAND ALI

Muhammad Ali is an icon. Ali knew his brand had a value from selling signed goods. For years the going rate was $25 and annually he might sign around 15,000 for profit, on tickets, posters, boxing gloves (that would sell for $200), statues and the like. He marketed sports collectibles through a company called Sports Placement Services, but he and his family had limited control of, and therefore limited earning power from, his wider brand, such as use of his face, of his names Cassius Clay and Muhammad Ali, and even phrases such as "Float like a butterfly, sting like a bee".

A copy of the book *Greatest Of All Time: A Tribute to Muhammad Ali* published by Taschen.

In 2006 Ali signed a $50 million deal with the Entertainment and licensing firm CKX. This was to form a new company G.O.A.T. LLC, which stands for "Greatest of All Time," in which Ali received 20 per cent and CKX 80 per cent from selling his name and likeness. CKX had many other 'partners with iconic content', including Elvis Presley's name and likeness, found on objects such as velvet paintings and commemorative shot glasses, Graceland, and the American Idol television series. Some of the first Ali-inspired goods were snack foods with names such as 'Rumble' and flavours including 'Thrill-A-Dill-A' and a limited edition luxury book. It was called *GOAT: A Tribute to Muhammad Ali*. Weighing 75 pounds (34 kg) with nearly 800 pages and more than 3,000 images of Ali and his life, it was covered in silk and Louis Vuitton leather and sold for $7,500.

In 2011, the brand giant IMG Licensing bought out G.O.A.T. and acquired the newly formed Muhammad Ali Enterprises and the Ali brand, which represents, "rebelliousness, excellence and inspiration in equal parts". Brand Ali is now in a stable that includes Ferrari, Dole bananas, World Series of Poker, and Goodyear tyres. In 2014, the first line of Adidas Muhammad Ali boxing apparel appeared in stores.

BIRTHDAY CELEBRATIONS

There were at least five parties to celebrate Muhammad Ali's 70th birthday but one of the biggest and most star-studded, was the "Power of Love Gala" on 18 February 2012, at the Grand Garden Arena, Las Vegas, the site of most of boxing's major fights in the last 20 years. Famous faces, including David Beckham, Anthony Hopkins and Samuel L Jackson, paid ticket prices starting at $1,500. The gala raised awareness about conditions such as Alzheimer's and Parkinson's Disease, and funds for the Cleveland Clinic Lou Ruvo Center for Brain Health and the Muhammad Ali Centre in Louisville. The event also raised funds through an auction, in which the pair of Ali's boxing gloves that he used to defeat Floyd Patterson in 1965, were sold for $1.1 million to Lorenzo Fertitta, a casino owner. A four-night stay at private islands in the Bahamas owned by magician David Copperfield raised $300,000.

During the 5-hour long birthday bash, the former heavyweight boxing champion was honoured by singers, athletes and actors who spoke and performed in tribute to Ali. Stevie Wonder sang Happy Birthday and there were also performances by Cee-Lo Green, Lenny Kravitz, Snoop Dogg, and LL Cool J, who rapped, "Mama Said Knock You Out". Footballer David Beckham paid tribute to Ali saying he was an inspiration and President Obama made an appearance via a heartfelt video message. The event was televised on 25 February and Samuel L Jackson told the audience: "He's done it with guts and grace, with his fists, and with his wits. He's one of the groundbreaking figures of the generation that helped make the world a more open place when it comes to who we can love, where we can go and what we can do."

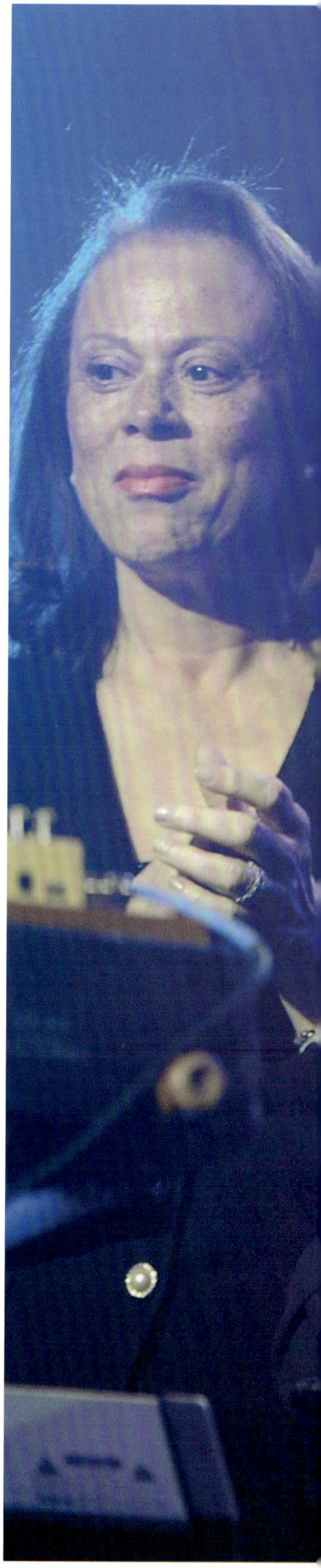

Lonnie, Ali and recording artist Sean "Diddy" Combs onstage during the Keep Memory Alive foundation's Power of Love Gala celebrating Ali's 70th birthday.

ALI TODAY

By 2014, there had been numerous stories about the possible demise of Muhammad Ali. In 2011, he was taken to hospital after falling unconscious soon after attending the funeral of Joe Frazier, where although frail, Ali had stood to energetically applaud his old adversary. In 2013, there were rumours he could no longer speak and was on the verge of death, but in response, Ali's family posted a picture of him watching the Superbowl on television and striking a defiant pose with boxing fists. A year later, in April 2014, Ali was pictured with boxer Andre Berto at his home in Arizona, where Berto reported that Ali had dished out pearls of wisdom such as "Stay focused on the task" and "Don't worry about the outside noise". As at many other times in his life, the Greatest appeared to be defying expectations and fighting on when he seemed to be down and out.

Ali is rarely seen at public events and spends much of his time at home nowadays, enjoying the family times he missed out on when he was boxing. Laila Ali, his daughter, said: "...he lights up when he sees the kids, especially my son who looks exactly like him. He loves that."

One of his latest, rare public appearances was in October 2013, at the inaugural Muhammad Ali Humanitarian Awards in Louisville, proving that he may be frail but his commitment to social justice has not diminished. While Parkinson's disease has taken a severe toll on Ali, his wife Lonnie said: "Every day he gets up with a smile in his face and looks forward to whatever the day brings. He doesn't let things stop him and he does as much as he can every day and he still finds meaning in life."

Ali and his daughter, Hana Yasmeen Ali, promoting his book, *The Soul of a Butterfly* in 2004 in New York.

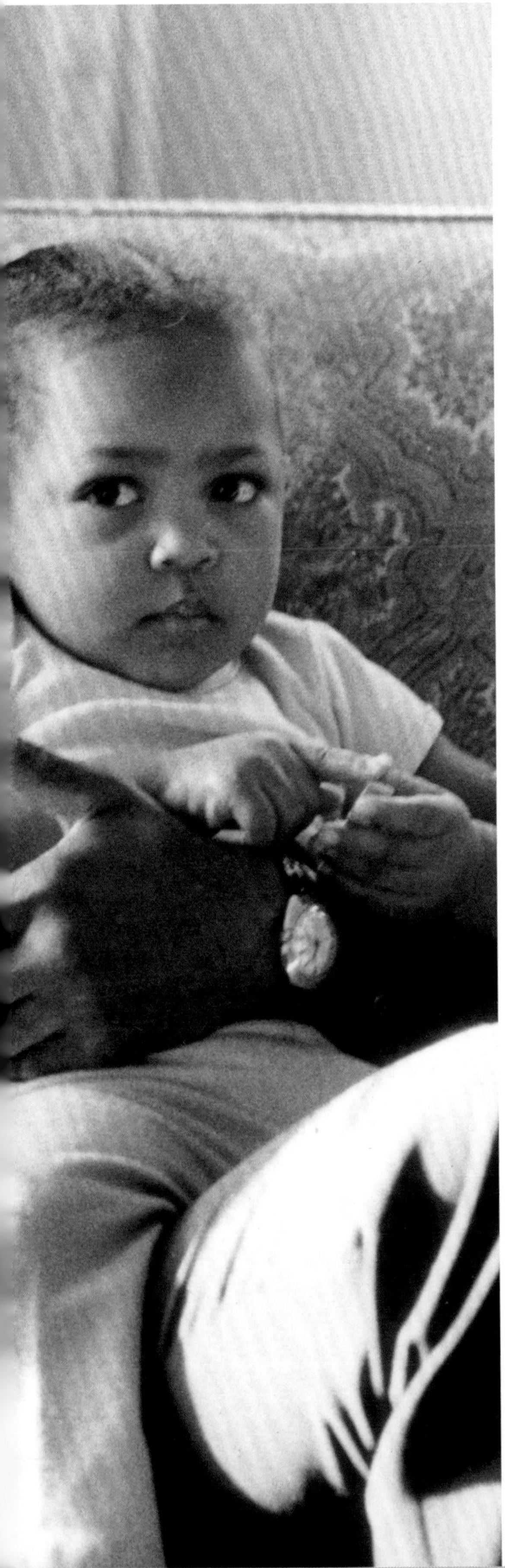

PERSONAL LIFE

Ali training for a fight in Munich while spending time with his twin daughters, Jamillah and Rasheda in 1971.

FAMILY LIFE

Being one of the most famous men on the planet and travelling as much as he did away from home must have made it difficult for Ali to maintain a home life. He has been married four times and has nine children: seven daughters and two sons. Two of his daughters, Miya (born 1971) and Khalilah (born 1974), were from affairs he had while married to his second wife, Belinda.

When Ali met 23-year-old Sonji Roi, she was working as a cocktail waitress. She was very beautiful and Ali was so taken with her that he proposed the night they met. They married in August 1964, first under Islamic law and then with a Justice of the Peace to make it legal under US law, but by June 1965 Ali filed for divorce. One reason stated was that Sonji refused to follow the religion of Islam as she had promised to, for example never wearing a headdress or veil. When the divorce was finalised on 10 January 1966, Ali sent her a note saying: "You traded Heaven for Hell, baby."

Ali met Belinda Boyd because her mother worked as a sort of companion for Elijah Muhammad's wife. They had a quiet private marriage ceremony in Chicago, after which Belinda changed her name to Khalilah Ali, although old friends and family continued to call her Belinda. She stayed in the background as she believed a Muslim wife should do and she and Ali had four children: Maryum (born 1968), twins Rasheeda and Jamillah (born 1970), and Muhammad Junior (1972). She recalled some of their happiest times were when the government stripped Ali of his title, and they travelled together to his lectures at colleges around the country and she managed their depleted finances.

Ali holds up his 4-month-old son Muhammad Ali, Jr., in 1972, outside his Deer Lake, PA, training camp.

BELINDA AND ALI BREAK UP

Ali and Belinda were married for almost ten years before their marriage broke up because of Ali's affair with Veronica Porsche. Veronica was one of four poster girls who helped to promote the 1974 Rumble in the Jungle fight. At first, Belinda turned a blind eye to the affair, believing Veronica was just, "one of the bunch", even allowing Veronica to join them on family trips, billed as the babysitter.

However, when Veronica accompanied Ali to Manila and met Ferdinand and Imelda Marcos before the big fight, she was introduced as his wife and Ali did not correct the error. Once the story broke, Ali tried to justify his need to have a girlfriend at a press conference and it became big news. Belinda flew straight to Manila and Ali's heated fight with her at his hotel became almost as big a story as the upcoming boxing match! Belinda finally admitted defeat and filed for divorce in 1976. She got a generous divorce settlement and Ali put $1 million in a trust fund for their four children.

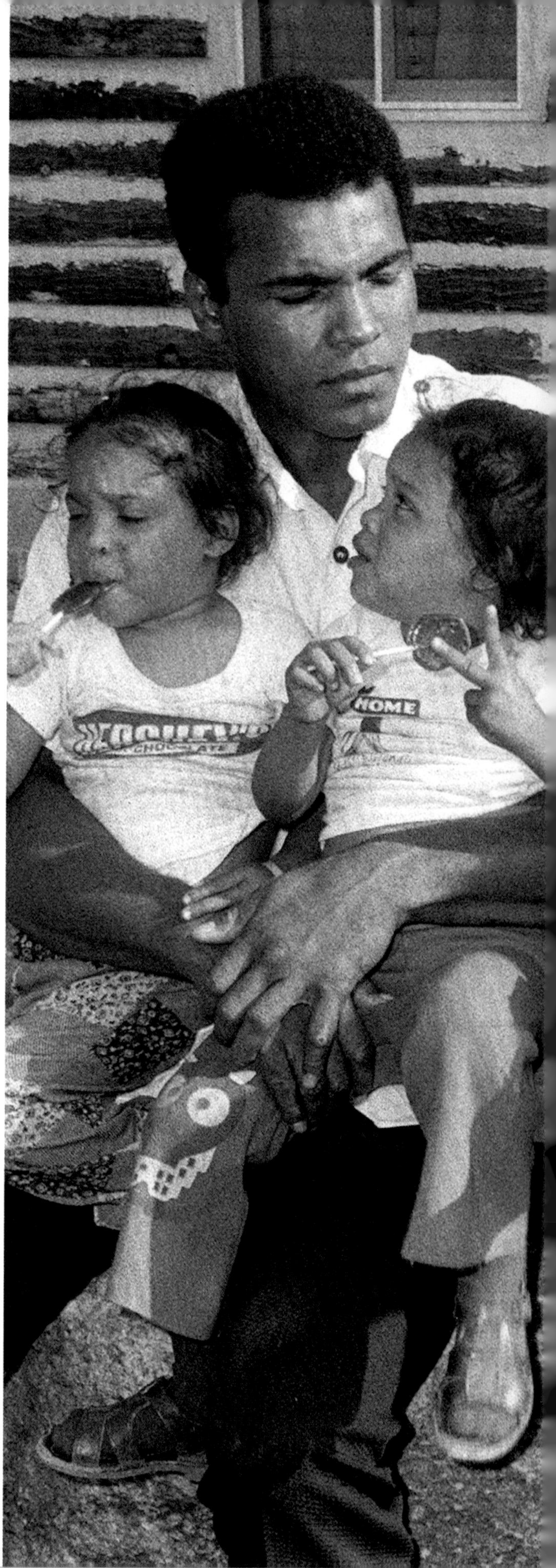

Ali with his second wife, Belinda, and three of their four children at Deer Lake, Pennsylvania, in August 1973.

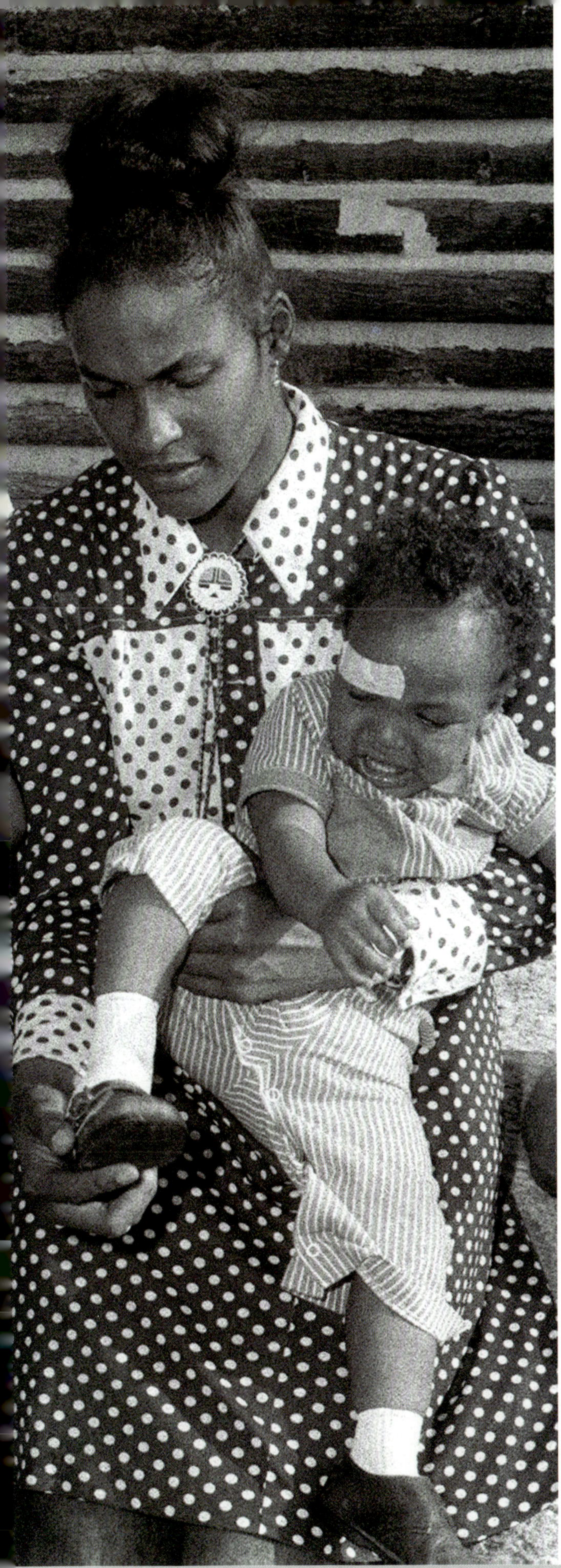

When Ali and Veronica got married on 19 June 1977 their first daughter, Hana (born 1976), was about ten months old and Veronica was pregnant with their second daughter, Laila Ali (born 1977). Veronica and Ali lived in luxury in a huge mansion in LA but the strain soon started to show on their relationship. Ali missed his busy life as a boxer and Veronica felt confined because while she wanted to continue her career, Ali wanted her to stay at home. By now Ali was also feeling tired all the time and his speech was slurred. On a visit home to Louisville in 1982 he met his fourth wife-to-be, Yolanda Williams, and by 1985, he and Veronica had filed for divorce.

Ali poses with his third wife Veronica outside his home at Freemont Place, Los Angeles in March 1982.

Ali with Lonnie Williams in Michigan, in July 1999.

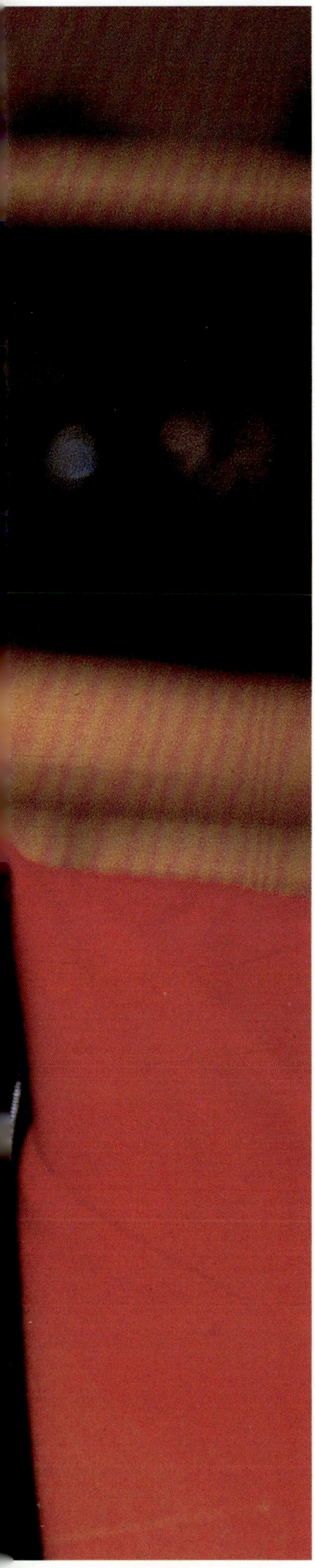

YOLANDA WILLIAMS

Ali married his fourth wife, Yolanda Williams, known as Lonnie, in 1986 but they first met back in 1962, when her family moved into a house opposite his, when she was five and he was 20. Her mother recalls Yolanda, like all the local kids, being in awe of him and Ali looking after her like an older brother. She recalled Ali playing driving around town before his fight with Sonny Liston in a bus with "Cassius Clay" written on the sides, with as many kids as would fit on it, him shouting: "Who's the Greatest!" and the kids calling back: "You are!"

When Lonnie and Ali met for lunch in 1982 she was studying for an MBA at Louisville University but was upset by the noticeable decline in his health, and, with Veronica's permission, moved to a house near his in LA to help to care for him and continue her studies there. She converted to Islam and when he divorced Veronica in 1986, she and Ali were married at a quiet ceremony in Louisville. His mother-in-law said this was an example of Ali not forgetting his roots: "A lot of people, when they get famous, they forget old friends, or at least they expect you to come to them. But not Muhammad." Ali and Lonnie are still together and have one son, Asaad Amin, whom they adopted when he was five months old.

Many people who know Ali and Lonnie say she is very good for Ali and that his physical and financial state stabilised after they got married. However, there is still some controversy. In 2014, Ali's eldest son, Muhammad Jr., accused Lonnie of making it difficult for him to see his father while he and his family live on the breadline in Chicago. A similar accusation was also made by Ali's brother, Rahman.

BOXER FOCUS: LAILA ALI

Laila Amaria Ali was born on 30 December 1977 in Miami Beach, Florida. She grew up in California with her parents Muhammad Ali and Veronica Porsche-Ali, and her older sister, Hana. During troubled teenage years, she spent time in a juvenile detention centre but afterwards, earned a degree in business management and owned a nail salon. She was inspired to become a boxer after seeing a televised fight between female boxers Christy Martin and Deirdre Gogarty in 1996.

Laila had first her professional fight on 8 October 1999, knocking out opponent April Fowler 31 seconds into round one. Over her career, she fought many leading names in women's boxing, including Jacqui Frazier-Lyde, daughter of boxer Joe Frazier, who she defeated in 2001 after a fight that was widely promoted as "Ali vs. Frazier IV". In 2002, she won the IBA title with a two-round knockout of Suzette Taylor and in November the same year, she retained that title and added the WIBA and IWBF belts, after an eight-round knockout win over world champion Valerie Mahfood. Laila retired from boxing in 2007 as undefeated Super Middleweight Boxing Champion of the World. Her ring nickname was "She Bee Stingin", a nod to her father's famous phrase, "Float like a butterfly, sting like a bee."

After retiring from boxing, Laila Ali has become a television host and personality, featuring in shows such *Dancing with the Stars* (2007), *American Gladiators* (2008) and *Stars Earn Stripes* (2012), *All in with Laila Ali* (2013) as well as exercise videos. She wrote a book, *Reach!* in 2002, and launched a range of beauty products. She is married to former NFL star Curtis Conway and they have two children, son Curtis Jr and daughter Sydney.

Laila Ali poses for a portrait in August 2001 in New York.

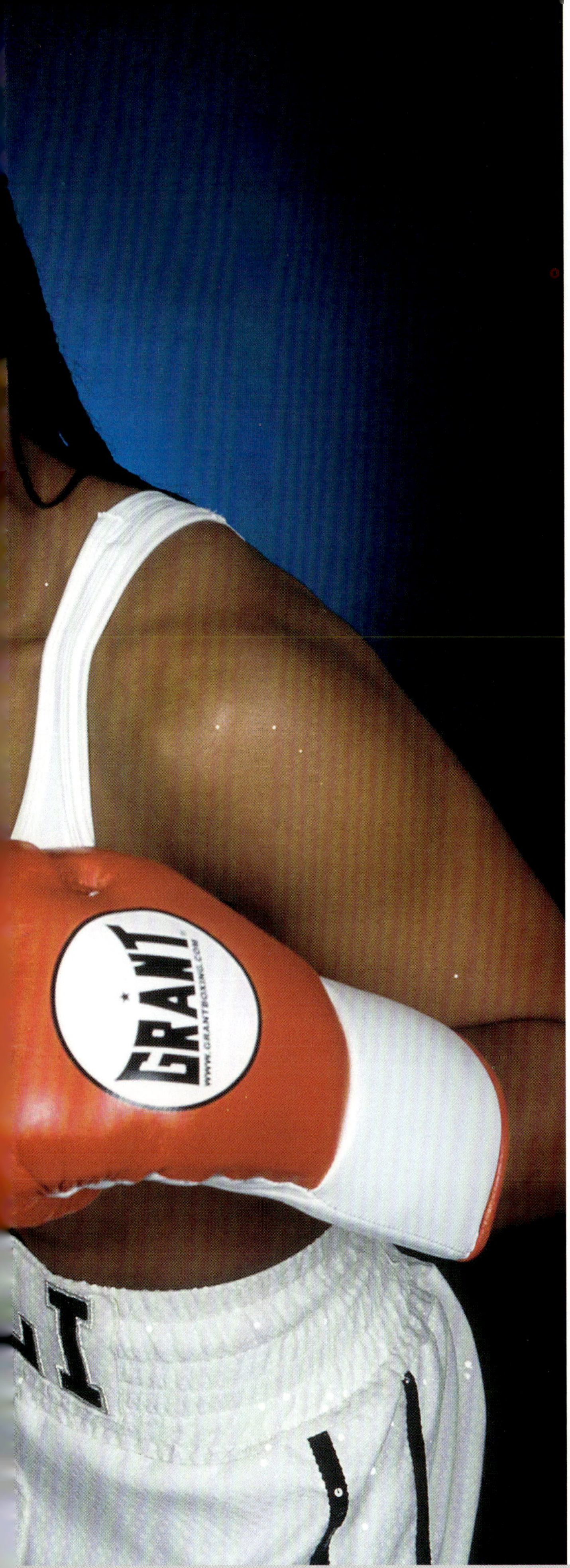

Laila Ali with her father, Muhammad Ali, after a WBC/WIBA Super Middleweight title bout in Washington, DC.

STATISTICS

BORN	Miami (FL), 30 December 1977
TURNED PROFESSIONAL	1999
NUMBER OF PRO BOUTS	24
WINS-LOSSES-DRAWS	24-0-0
NUMBER OF KNOCKOUTS	21
RETIRED	2007

Ali prays at the Alabaster Mosque in Cairo, Egypt in October 1986.

RELIGIOUS LIFE

A belief in one God, who created everything in the universe, has been the driving force in Muhammad Ali's long life, although his religious views have developed over time. After he began to study the Quran in the mid-1970s, he converted from his mother's Baptist religion to become a follower of Islam. He joined the Nation of Islam, an organisation that combined elements of traditional Islam with black nationalist ideas, and followed the teachings of Elijah Muhammad, who proclaimed all white people were 'devils' who hated black people and that it was time for black people to unite and assert themselves. Ali was vilified by the press and the white establishment for his change of religion and the change of name that came with it.

In 1972, Ali began to turn from the Nation of Islam to a mainstream Sunni Islam faith. In this year, he also made his first hajj, or pilgrimage, to Mecca, wearing the correct orthodox ihram attire. He began to pray five times a day and to fast during Ramadan. Ali himself expressed a broader tolerance and acceptance that other religions contain truth too: "Rivers, ponds, lakes and streams – they all have different names, but they all contain water. Just as religions do – they all contain truths." He also said that no matter what religion you believe in, if you live a good life you'll receive God's blessing and go to heaven.

In 1975, Elijah Muhammad died and when his son Wallace D Mohammed became leader of the Nation of Islam, he, like Malcolm X before him, also converted to orthodox Islam and most Nation of Islam members followed him. The Nation of Islam was eventually known as the American Society of Muslims and welcomed people of all races, too.

In 2005, according to Ali's daughter, Hana, Ali embraced spiritual practices of Sufism, a mystical branch or sect of Islam, after reading Sufi teachings in a collection of books by a man named Hazrat Inayat Khan. Sufism is a belief and practice in which Muslims seek to find the truth of divine love and knowledge through direct personal experience of God.

In his later years, Ali has seen himself primarily as a holy man. He published a memoir entitled *The Soul of a Butterfly: Reflections on Life's Journey,* which he wrote over the course of two years with his daughter Hana. It is an unconventional autobiography that combines reminiscences with stories, poems, and spiritual lessons, and in which he discusses the meaning of religion. He is also the co-author of *Healing: A Journal of Tolerance and Understanding* and *The Greatest: My Own Story.*

His religious beliefs gave him the values that shaped and sustained him and continued to guide him throughout his life. In his later years, it has become much harder for Ali to follow strictly the daily pattern of the call to prayer, but he still prays or reads when he can, saying that although his physical abilities were taken from him, he was given something greater: a chance to focus completely on his journey to forgiveness and peace.

Ali sums up his belief in spirituality best in his own words: "The only true satisfaction comes from honouring and worshipping God. Being a true Muslim is the most important thing in the world to me. It means more to me than being black or being American. I can't save other people's souls: only God can do that. But I can try to save my own."

Ali watches a basketball game between the Phoenix Suns and Miami Heat at US Airways Center, Phoenix, in 2010.

THE ALI LEGACY

Float Like
A BUTTER FLY
Sting Like
A BEE

Ali and fellow boxing legend Lennox Lewis pose with television presenter Harry Carpenter at the BBC Sports Personality of the Year Awards in London in 1999.

INSPIRING ATHLETES

Muhammad Ali was an outstanding athlete, who inspired generations of sportsmen and women around the world to follow their dreams. Of course, many of the athletes inspired by his determination and success, are from the world of boxing, such as Lennox Lewis, who said: "Muhammad Ali inspired me – from when I was a young boy growing up – he motivated me to chase my dreams inside and out of the ring."

Ali is also an inspiration for athletes from other sports disciplines and to both men and women. Footballer David Beckham has said of Ali: "Muhammad Ali has shown us one man can make a difference. His example of love, character, dignity, makes us want to be better." US tennis star Serena Williams said that she was inspired by Ali's fighting spirit not to give up after she struggled to get back on form after recovering from a blood clot on her lungs in 2011.

In December 1999, as the 20th century drew to a close, Ali was awarded no fewer than three Sportsman of the Century awards. He won the Sports Illustrated Athlete of the Century Award, the World Sports Award's World Sportsman of the Century and the BBC Sports personality of the century, in which he had garnered more votes than all of the other four candidates put together. Other legendary sportspeople were shortlisted for all awards, including Brazilian football star Pele and US tennis player Pete Sampras, whose sporting successes had no doubt equalled Ali's. Once again it was Ali's compelling skill, style, personality and his campaigning for causes he believed in, which made him stand out above the others. Ali collected the Sports Illustrated award at New York's Madison Square Garden, in front of many of the world's greatest athletes who gave him a standing ovation.

US tennis star Serena Williams is just one of many athletes who have been inspired by Ali's sporting skills and determination in some way.

INSPIRING ACTION

Muhammad Ali is more than an inspiring athlete. He is also a role model who encouraged people to stand up for what they believe in and to use their positions of privilege for positive action. After Australian Aboriginal sprinter Nova Peris-Kneebone presented Ali with the Olympic torch at Sydney in 2000, she explained that meeting him was important to her because, like Ali standing up for civil rights in the US, she used her celebrity to promote Aboriginal health and other issues in Australia. Standing with Ali at a press event, she said: "If you believe in something strong enough and you go out and stand for it, people start to take notice," at which point Ali said: "She's telling the truth."

Jack Newfield in *The Nation* magazine said Ali believed that if he fought he could persuade others to do so, too: "Ali believed that if he could beat Liston or Foreman or Frazier, that would inspire a junkie to get off drugs, a child to survive a terminal illness, a welfare recipient to get a job, a drunk to go to rehab. He believed his life could change other lives..."

Ali has also inspired leaders of nations. In 2005, President George Bush awarded Ali the United States' highest civilian honour, the Presidential Medal of Freedom. One year earlier and four years before being elected the first ever black US president, Barack Obama wrote about how Ali inspired him in an essay for a special edition of *USA Today:* "This is the Muhammad Ali who inspires us today – the man who believes real success comes when we rise after we fall; who has shown us that through undying faith and steadfast love, each of us can make this world a better place. He is, and always will be, the champ." Ali's picture is a reminder of this inspiration hanging in pride of place on the White House wall.

Ali never stops playing to the crowds! Here he is making a humorous gesture to George W. Bush after receiving the Presidential Medal of Freedom in 2005.

Picture Credits

4–5 Phil Greitzer/NY Daily News Archive via Getty Images; 6–7 Keystone-France/Gamma-Keystone via Getty Images; 8–9 Express/Archive Photos/Getty Images; 10 Charles 'Teenie' Harris/Carnegie Museum of Art/Getty Images; 11 AFP/Getty Images; 12–13 Jack Delano/Getty Images; 14 Buyenlarge/Getty Images; 15 New York Times Co./Getty Images; 16–17 Popperfoto/Getty Images; 18–19 FPG/Getty Images; 20 AFP/Getty Images; 20–21 Keystone-France/Gamma-Keystone via Getty Images; 22–23 The Ring Magazine/Getty Images; 24 NY Daily News Archive via Getty Images; 25 Frank Hurley/NY Daily News Archive via Getty Images; 26–27 Central Press/Getty Images; 28–29 Focus on Sport/Getty Images; 30 Tony Triolo/Sports Illustrated/Getty Images; 32–33 James Drake/Time & Life Pictures/Getty Images; 33 James Drake/Time & Life Pictures/Getty Images; 35 James Drake/Time & Life Pictures/Getty Images; 36 Ray Fisher/Time Life Pictures/Getty Images; 37 Focus on Sport/Getty Images; 38–39 Ron Case/Keystone/Getty Images; 39 Keystone/Getty Images; 40 Lee Balterman/Sports Illustrated/Getty Images; 42 Tony Triolo/Sports Illustrated/Getty Images; 43 Tony Triolo/Sports Illustrated/Getty Images; 44¬–45 Doug McKenzie/Hulton Archive/Getty Images; 45 John Pratt/Keystone Features/Hulton Archive/Getty Images; 46–47 Keystone-France/Gamma-Keystone via Getty Images; 48–49 OLDPIX/ANSA/UIG/Getty Images; 50–51 The Ring Magazine/Getty Images; 51 George Silk/Time Life Pictures/Getty Images; 52–53 Herb Scharfman/Time Life Pictures/Getty Images; 54 Popperfoto/Getty Images; 55 James Drake /Time & Life Pictures/Getty Images; 56–57 Popperfoto/Getty Images; 58–59 NY Daily News Archive via Getty Images; 60 John Peodincuk/NY Daily News Archive via Getty Images; 61 Gerry Cranham/Sports Illustrated/Getty Images; 62 Universal History Archive/UIG via Getty images; 63 Buyenlarge/Getty Images; 64 John Dominis/Time & Life Pictures/ Getty Images; 65 The Ring Magazine/Getty Images; 66–67 Frank Castoral/NY Daily News Archive via Getty Images; 68–69 Central Press/Getty Images; 69 Popperfoto/Getty Images; 70–71 The Sydney Morning Herald/Fairfax Media via Getty Images; 72 Underwood Archives/Getty Images; 73 James Drake/Sports Illustrated/Getty Images; 74–75 David R. Lutman/Getty Images; 76–77 Joe Farrington/NY Daily News Archive via Getty Images; 78 The Ring Magazine/Getty Images; 80–81 Walter Kelleher/NY Daily News Archive via Getty Images; 81 Charles Hoff/NY Daily News Archive via Getty Images; 82 John Dominis/Time & Life Pictures/Getty Images; 83 Bob Gomel/Time Life Pictures/Getty Images; 84–85 Popperfoto/Getty Images; 86 Anwar Hussein/Getty Images; 87 Underwood Archives/Getty Images; 88–89 American Stock/Getty Images; 89 The Ring Magazine/Getty Images; 90–91 AFP/Getty Images; 92 Anthony Casale/NY Daily News Archive via Getty Images; 93 The Ring Magazine/ Getty Images; 94 Evening Standard/Getty Images; 94–95 AFP/Getty Images; 96 AFP/Getty Images; 97 AFP/Getty Images; 98–99 Tony Triolo/Sports Illustrated/Getty Images; 100 Rolls Press/Popperfoto/ Getty Images; 101 AFP/Getty Images; 102–103 Popperfoto/Getty Images; 103 The Ring Magazine/Getty Images; 104 Dieter LUDWIG/Gamma-Rapho via Getty Images; 105 Neil Leifer/Sports Illustrated/ Getty Images; 106 Rolls Press/Popperfoto/Getty Images; 107 Rolls Press/Popperfoto/Getty Images; 108–109 Neil Leifer/Sports Illustrated/Getty Images; 110–111 Focus on Sport/Getty Images; 112 AFP/Getty Images; 112–113 Herb Scharfman/Sports Imagery/Getty Images; 114–115 Takeo Tanuma/Sports Illustrated/Getty Images; 116 Popperfoto/Getty Images; 117 John Iacono/Sports Illustrated/ Getty Images; 118–119 The Ring Magazine/Getty Images; 119 The Ring Magazine/Getty Images; 120–121 Focus on Sport/Getty Images; 122–123 The Ring Magazine/Getty Images; 123 Tim Chapman; 124–125 Manny Millan/Sports Illustrated/Getty Images; 126–127 John Iacono/Sports Illustrated/Getty Images; 128–129 Robert Riger/Getty Images; 130–131 Time & Life Pictures/Getty Images; 132–133 Peter Charlesworth/LightRocket via Getty Images; 135 The Ring Magazine/Getty Images; 136–137 MARIA BASTONE/AFP/Getty Images; 139 Michael Cooper/Getty Images; 140–141 Paula Bronstein/ UNICEF/Getty Images; 141 Richard Corkery/NY Daily News Archive via Getty Images; 142–143 STEPHEN JAFFE/AFP/Getty Images; 144–145 Mike Moore/Getty Images for Fight Night; 146–147 LUCY NICHOLSON/AFP/Getty Images; 147 Peter Brandt/Getty Images; 148 JEFF HAYNES/AFP/Getty Images; 149 Dennis Macdonald/Photolibrary/Getty Images; 150 FABIAN MATZERATH/AFP/Getty Images; 151 Michael Buckner/Getty Images for Baby2Baby; 152–153 Ethan Miller/Getty Images for Keep Memory Alive; 154–155 Kramer/Getty Images; 156–157 Frank Tewkesbury/Evening Standard/ Getty Images; 158 Central Press/Getty Images; 159 Popperfoto/Getty Images; 160–161 Popperfoto/Getty Images; 161 AFP/Getty Images; 162–163 Steve Liss/Time Life Pictures/Getty Images; 164–165 The Ring Magazine/Getty Images; 165 Ed Mulholland/WireImage/Getty Images; 166 MIKE NELSON/AFP/Getty Images; 168–169 John W. McDonough/Sports Illustrated/Getty Images; 170–171 Anwar Hussein/Getty Images; 172 Craig Prentis/Allsport; 173 Mike Hewitt/Getty Images; 174–175 MANDEL NGAN/AFP/Getty Images

Endpapers: front left NY Daily News/Getty Images; front right Popperfoto/Getty Images; back left Popperfoto/Getty Images; back right NY Daily News/Getty Images
Cover: front Focus On Sport/Getty Images; back Thinkstock/Getty Images

Smok
Joe
MUHAMMAD
ALI